WRITING POLICY IN ACTION

Open University Press

English, Language, and Education series

General Editor: Anthony Adams
Lecturer in Education, University of Cambridge

TITLES IN THE SERIES

Narrative and Argument
Richard Andrews (ed.)

The Problem with Poetry
Richard Andrews

Writing Development
Roslyn Arnold

Writing Policy in Action
Eve Bearne and Cath Farrow

Time for Drama
Roma Burgess and Pamela Gaudry

Readers, Texts, Teachers
Bill Corcoran and Emrys Evans (eds)

Thinking Through English
Paddy Creber

Developing Response to Poetry
Patrick Dias and Michael Hayhoe

Developing English
Peter Dougill (ed.)

The Primary Language Book
Peter Dougill and Richard Knott

Children Talk About Books
Donald Fry

Literary Theory and English Teaching
Peter Griffith

Lesbian and Gay Issues in the English Classroom
Simon Harris

Reading and Response
Mike Hayhoe and Stephen Parker (eds)

Assessing English
Brian Johnston

Lipservice: The Story of Talk in Schools
Pat Jones

The English Department in a Changing World
Richard Knott

Oracy Matters
Margaret MacLure, Terry Phillips and Andrew Wilkinson (eds)

Language Awareness for Teachers
Bill Mittins

Beginning Writing
John Nichols *et al.*

Teaching Literature for Examinations
Robert Protherough

Developing Response to Fiction
Robert Protherough

Microcomputers and the Language Arts
Brent Robinson

Young People Reading
Charles Sarland

English Teaching from A–Z
Wayne Sawyer, Anthony Adams and Ken Watson

Reconstructing 'A' Level English
Patrick Scott

School Writing
Yanina Sheeran and Douglas Barnes

Reading Narrative as Literature
Andrew Stibbs

Collaboration and Writing
Morag Styles (ed.)

Reading Within and Beyond the Classroom
Dan Taverner

Reading for Real
Barrie Wade (ed.)

English Teaching in Perspective
Ken Watson

The Quality of Writing
Andrew Wilkinson

The Writing of Writing
Andrew Wilkinson (ed.)

Spoken English Illuminated
Andrew Wilkinson, Alan Davies and Deborah Berrill

WRITING POLICY IN ACTION

The middle years

**Eve Bearne and
Cath Farrow**

Open University Press
Milton Keynes · Philadelphia

Open University Press
Celtic Court
22 Ballmoor
Buckingham
MK18 1XW

and
1900 Frost Road, Suite 101
Bristol, PA 19007, USA

First Published 1991

Copyright © Eve Bearne and Cath Farrow 1991

All rights reserved. No part of this publication may be
reproduced, stored in a retrieval system or transmitted
in any form or by any means, without written permission
from the publisher.

British Library Cataloguing in Publication Data

Bearne, Eve
  Writing policy in action: The middle years.
  – (English language and education)
  I. Title. II. Farrow, Cath. III. Series
  372.6

  ISBN 0–335–09444–9

Library of Congress Cataloging-in-Publication Data

Bearne, Eve, 1943–
    Writing policy in action: the middle years/Eve Bearne & Cath Farrow.
    p.   cm. – (English, language, and education series)
    Includes index.
    ISBN 0–335–09444–9
    1. English language – Composition and exercises – Study and teaching
(Secondary) – Great Britain – Case studies.   2. English language –
Composition and exercises – Great Britain – Evaluation – Case studies.
    I. Farrow, Cath, 1938– . II. Title. III. Series.
LB1631.B36   1991
808′.042′0712 – dc20   91–14732
                                                                     CIP

Typeset by Type Study, Scarborough
Printed in Great Britain by Biddles Limited, Guildford and Kings Lynn

Contents

Acknowledgements vii
General editor's introduction ix

1 The development of writing: policy into practice 1
Time past, time present and time future 4
Perceptions of writing 5
Describing progress 8
Building up knowledge about language 13
The wider view 16
Going deeper 18
Partnerships for writing 20
Evaluation and assessment 22
Notes 24

2 Starting points 27
A framework for analysis 28
How much difference does context make? 31
Tracing experiences of literacy 34
Selecting writing for assessment 36
A wider range of writing analysed 37
'Disposable' writing – or is it? 41
Writers write about writing . . . 43
. . . and about being readers 45
Issues of content . . . and discontent 48
A clearer view of progress 52
The circle of literacy 55
Notes 56

3 The writing environment 58
Setting the scene 58

	Teachers as facilitators	60
	Teachers as readers	62
	Children as evaluators	69
	Notes	75
4	**A year's progress**	76
	Different writing experiences	78
	What do we do with writing?	79
	Passing on information	81
	Making the final comments	92
	Notes	95
5	**Children learning to think about writing**	96
	'I'd like to put the sentences in order'	98
	The importance of genre	103
	A circular argument?	107
	'When we put our own ideas into action'	111
	Notes	113
6	**Conclusion: putting the policy together**	115
	Start by talking	117
	Discover perceptions	119
	Recognize existing (good) practice	119
	Review and evaluate	120
	Focus on detail	122
	Record progress	123
	Put into a wider context	124
	Notes	125
	Appendix: Records of Achievement in Writing	129
	Index	160

Acknowledgements

There are, quite literally, thousands of children and adults to whom we owe our thanks. This book is a testament to the experience and commitment of all those people who were involved in the National Writing Project, most particularly those in Hampshire. Val Rowe, Headteacher of Burnham Copse Junior School, all the children who let us use their writing, Sue Phillips, Belinda Kerfoot-Roberts, Helen Maguire and Yvonne Ryves have shown great generosity in allowing us to write about what was, after all, *their* work! Other friends and colleagues have patiently and painstakingly read and responded to early drafts, helping us reflect on our own writing. Tony Adams has been a sympathetic and stimulating editor. And, perhaps most of all, we owe our thanks to Peter and Mick for providing the background support.

General editor's introduction

This book is one of the many outcomes following the National Writing Project classroom research on which Eve Bearne worked with her colleague, Cath Farrow. In their detailed account of a particular school and the writing that took place inside it, the two authors give a unique perspective on the writing process. There have been, of course, detailed studies of individual writing in the past, especially by American and Canadian writers, but, generally, these have dealt with small and rather carefully selected groups of students. In its exploration of a typical classroom context, seen from the twin perspectives of the researcher and the teacher, this book breaks new ground and conveys to the reader a powerful sense of immediacy and authenticity. The progress of individual writers' explorations of their growing craft comes powerfully off the page and it was this that first attracted me to the proposal for the book.

Especially at the time when, in England and Wales, we are introducing a National Curriculum calling for careful monitoring of student progress by the classroom teacher this book will be found most helpful. It shows how such monitoring can take place without becoming burdensome on the teacher and how students' writing can be encouraged and enhanced by the constructive use of formative writing profiles.

Readers of other books in this series will notice that the present volume is in many ways complementary to that by Rosalyn Arnold drawing upon her research experience in Australia. The publication of the two books in close proximity in the series was a deliberate choice since they share a common concern for developing the young writer and show how across the world certain ways of teaching writing have proved fruitful.

At the time of writing this introduction I am visiting a large number of schools to observe English students on teaching practice. I am particularly impressed by how, already in 1991, the National Curriculum is having its effect on work in writing going on in schools, especially in the area of drafting and redrafting. Lip service has, of course, been paid to the skills of drafting in the past; there are now signs that this vital part of the writing process is being taken seriously by both students and teachers.

Those seeking practical help in guiding the young writer's progress through the writing process will find it in plenty in these pages. They will also have the privilege of becoming intimates of the classroom that the two writers describe and realize that learning to become a writer is a longitudinal process in which the climate for writing is of paramount importance.

Case study research is well established in educational circles. The present volume is a distinguished contribution to the field.

Anthony Adams

1 The development of writing: policy into practice

'What is your policy about writing?' A daunting question and one which begs several other questions before it can be given a satisfactory answer. A first response to such a challenge might be to produce the school's written policy, to demonstrate that it has been given some thought and has been recorded as an agreed document. But is this really the policy about writing which all the teachers in the school use every day when they work with their classes? It may be. What is more likely is that it represents just a fraction of the regular practice of teachers and the daily experience of children. What is also likely is that since the policy was written down, some of those practices and experiences will have shifted and developed. That is what teaching and learning are like.

This is not to suggest that there should be no school policy about writing, or about language. Shared understandings are important in any school. What is clear, though, is that a policy, be it about writing, mathematics, science or technology, does not only exist as a written statement. It is a set of live and active practices. And this is the strength of any thought-out, discussed, negotiated and agreed set of principles. They are still alive even when they have been captured on paper. Their written form represents a point in the history and development of a set of shared ideas. At best these ideas will have come from quite a lengthy debate – even disagreement – among a group of colleagues who are intent on forging a way of working with children which will challenge and support them as they move towards some measure of independence in learning. At worst, the policy will have been hastily written down by one person who has been landed with the job, to satisfy an external demand for 'something on paper', and after that individual's strenuous efforts it will simply gather dust on a shelf. This is the difference between a policy in action which expresses lived and living experience of writing and a purposeless exercise done simply to satisfy someone else.

This book is about policy in action. Being able to describe, analyse and assess children's development as writers means that teachers have some sense of how best to help children progress both as writers and learners. Setting up the classroom conditions which will best foster development is a way of making a policy real.

What is interesting is that the description of different approaches to policy-making can equally be applied to writing in schools. Traditionally, classroom writing used to be done to satisfy external demands – to prove that something had been done or simply to check up on children's abilities. More recently the emphasis has shifted towards giving attention to writing as a process or as a way for children to work out ideas. In other words, classroom writing used to be seen as a 'thing', complete and existing as evidence that the writer knew something: either the facts contained in the writing or how to present technically correct work. This often meant that children had to produce a piece of writing in a set time, about a given topic, and that this would be seen as a finished product, assessed and marked as an indicator of what they had learned and as proof of technical competence. More recently, however, this view of writing as a noun – a 'thing' – has changed. Attention has been given to writing as a verb – an activity – something in the process of construction which should be read for the meaning it carries, as an indication of the writer's ideas and personal intentions to convince, entertain, give opinions, and suggesting the developing writer's potential for future achievements as well as past. From there it becomes a focus for discussion as young writers learn strategies for revision and self-editing.

Looked at like this, the parallels between developing policy and developing writing become clearer. Just as we have come to understand that children achieve more when they are aware of the reasons for writing and see it as having some meaning for themselves, so we can understand from our own daily experience as teachers that we are at our most effective when we are clear about why we are doing certain activities with the children rather than others, and when we can operate according to experience which is based on considered principles. Just as children will often commit themselves more strenuously to careful revising, editing and redrafting when they see writing as having some meaning for them, expressing their own thoughts, beliefs and feelings, so teachers will whole-heartedly spend time working on ideas which satisfy their own demands and questions.

Put like that it sounds quite straightforward, quite easy to achieve; but of course it is not! There are always constraints and complexities which have to be worked through before the point is genuinely reached where both classroom writing and teachers' policy-making can be seen as actively developing. This book is intended to look at some of these complications and to suggest possible ways of coping with the constraints.

In the following chapters we describe how teachers in one school have explored possibilities for a detailed analysis of writing development. At the same time they have been finding ways of establishing classroom practices which offer possibilities for young writers to develop their capabilities in all areas of the curriculum which will satisfy the demands of personal learning as well as those of the National Curriculum. Work was going on in several classes at the same time.

In trying to describe some of the issues raised by the teachers' classroom investigations, we have selected particular aspects as 'snapshots' of their work. These accounts are not offered as a blueprint or a set of 'rules' which will necessarily lead to success. Readers will be able to recognize some shared ideas and, we hope, to challenge others. Two underlying threads guide our descriptions of what these teachers did.

First, developing a policy for writing and learning has to be the result of teachers' own questions, explorations and thought. Other people can offer ideas and suggestions, but they cannot dictate the routes which each individual teacher will take to establish a more productive and satisfying classroom approach to writing.

Second, teachers know more than they think they know! The work outlined here is not offered as 'expert' advice, but as the beginnings of a dialogue between the ideas used by the teachers whose work makes up this book and the experiences of other informed and knowledgeable colleagues who will be reading it.

The work, as we present it here, begins with a detailed study in the following chapter of some individual pieces of writing by 11-year-olds in Sue Phillips' class who were shortly to leave their primary school. This close focus indicates some features of development and provides a touchstone for a broader study of the classroom conditions and teacher interventions which contributed to their abilities both as writers and learners. The question we ask is, if we can say that these children are competent writers, just how did they get to that level of competence? Chapter 3 goes back to look at a class of children who are at a much earlier stage in their school experience, tracking the ways in which Cath Farrow, their teacher, builds an environment which helps them become more confident and competent writers, readers and talkers. The later chapters take a broader perspective, looking in some detail at the progress of two competent writers in Cath's class during the course of a year, then going on to consider how less confident writers in a parallel class were supported and encouraged. Finally, to come full-circle, we look back at writing by the same children who, as 11-year-olds, began our study. This time, though, the writing comes from their second year in the Junior school. From these separate 'snapshots' we hope to sketch out a picture of progress.

First, then, in this 'case study' of a school working on its writing policy, we looked in detail at some examples of children's texts in order to define features which might be taken as indicators of the 'growing ability' in writing described in the National Curriculum for England and Wales. We then considered ways in which children can be helped to develop their writing through planned and consistent classroom practice. Both of these ways of looking at children's writing development led to teachers using the insights gained to begin to flesh out a way of observing and keeping written records of children's progress as writers. The simple and effective method described not only is a useful way of involving children in tracking their own development but also forms a basis for thinking about what ought to be included in a full writing curriculum.

This is not, then, a book which describes a 'scientific' study of writing. There are no quantifiable data. There are, however, careful studies of texts and classroom practice which allow some generalizations to be made about how we might best describe writing development in the years from 7 to 11 and, most importantly, how teachers can most fruitfully promote children's writing abilities. In presenting a picture of a school in a small town with a reasonably mixed population in terms of occupation, we are emphatically not suggesting this as a model or a pattern. What we hope to offer is a description which may have some relevance to readers in all sorts of other areas and other schools,[1] as well as some points of contact and some areas for debate and disagreement. Above all, we hope to present a way of looking at writing which might raise a few questions about how teachers can help their pupils make the most of their language capabilities.

Time past, time present and time future

Looking way back at the history of writing, it is clear that people began to make marks to record things because they felt they needed to. As societies became more developed, speech was captured in written symbols to answer a variety of practical and personal needs. Although there are complex social groups in many parts of the world who still use oral language as the main, and perfectly satisfying, means of communication, writing has nevertheless become embedded in the fabric of history. Its significance, importance and the values attached to it have become historically developed and enshrined within social practice. Writing has political significance. This book does not deal with that kind of political history and analysis; it is about the living histories of teachers and children in schools today where writing, as a major means of learning, has implications and importance in the continuing histories of schools and the communities within and around them.

Put briefly, writing matters. It matters in school and outside it. It matters as a means of individual expression and as it reflects the diverse cultures and communities from which our children come. It matters because of the way it is understood in the larger social organization of the country. In terms of how writing is approached in schools it is important because of its potential in allowing or inhibiting learning in all areas of the curriculum. What children bring to learning – their past personal, cultural and literacy experiences – combines with present classroom experience and suggests future possibilities for literacy and learning. If the classroom is a place where past experience can be recognized and valued, where writing can use the energy of children's language, taking the risks involved, then there is a chance to map future progress. Part of any policy for writing has to take account of the language capabilities which children bring with them when they enter the classroom.

This is all very well, but how can it be done? What about the daily workload, frustrations and anxieties which get in the way? This is neither the time nor the place for pious platitudes but for practicality. What we hope to show in this book are some possible ways in which principles can be made real in practice, on a daily, weekly, termly, yearly basis; ways in which they can be seen working as active policy and which might, in the end, offer some resolution to the conflicting demands being made on teachers. There are, however, no easy answers. Anyone who has taken the risk of developing different classroom approaches will know that it can be unnerving. Anyone who has tried something new will recognize that learning takes time and it is often only when looking back that it becomes clear how far you have come.

The metaphor of a journey is a useful one. The work and ideas which we outline here represent a pause on the way; a chance to look at the map and see which might now be a sensible direction to take. Suggesting ways of looking at children's writing and classroom approaches which help children themselves to read their own writing attentively and critically, represents what has already happened, where the teachers and children involved in the work we describe here have come from. Offering ways of recording and assessing children's progress in writing suggests possible future directions. The terrain is laid down, by the history of writing in schools and by the demands of the National Curriculum and by the practical necessities of everyday life in the classroom. Describing one route which has been taken need not mean that there is only one way of travelling through this complicated territory. In fact, we intend quite the opposite. In outlining how particular teachers and children have found some ways through we want emphatically to urge that anyone who reads this book will use the ideas as an opportunity to find their own routes through this varied landscape. But before this metaphor is completely overworked, it is necessary to describe the history and geography of the land – to outline some of the past experiences of writing in schools and to look at what development in writing might mean.

Perceptions of writing

Since the beginning of statutory schooling for all (and probably before) strange things have happened to people's perceptions of what writing is. If any ordinary family today had a look at the kinds of writing which happen in the home during a month or so, they would find an interesting variety of reasons for writing.[2] There would be shopping lists or lists of jobs to be done; notes to other members of the family, neighbours or regular callers at the house; letters, both personal and formal; crosswords, competitions and wordgames; diaries or memories written in photograph albums; more lengthy writing for school or for work; sometimes there are records of local meetings, stories and poems. The reasons for reading and talking will be equally varied. The language environment in any home is far richer and more diverse than we often recognize – even in those homes where there appears to be little evidence of formal literacy. Writing will be seen in many different forms, too: kept as letters; displayed on the kitchen wall as children's first efforts at making meaning; in diaries, telephone books, address books; in newsprint and computer printout; in books and magazines; in leaflets posted through the door; in files, folders and albums. But how far is this variety in the purposes for writing and the forms writing can take reflected in the classroom?

In some classrooms, of course, there will be just as many different forms of writing in evidence. Often, however, there is a more narrow range where writing is seen primarily in exercise books and the reasons for writing are not to answer the needs or purposes of all members of the classroom community but to satisfy other criteria. This is not an exaggerated picture, as children's own comments reveal. When the children at one junior school were asked by their teachers 'Why do you write?' their answers were illuminating. There were the ones who understood something about writing as communication – with oneself or other people:

> I write to my gran to keep in touch
>
> to send invitations to friends
>
> secret diary

There were others who seemed to understand that writing helps you learn:

> to do my maths
>
> so I can remember things
>
> to show the teacher what I've done

But there were some whose views of writing were either chilling or showed considerable confusion:

> punishment
>
> teacher says so
>
> if we didn't write we'd waste paper[3]

It is perhaps best not to exaggerate the importance of these last replies. But even taking the comments as not entirely representative, two significant points emerge. The first concerns the difference between children's views of writing at home and at school. Writing done at home was seen as having meaning in terms of communication or pleasure – to satisfy personal intentions. Writing at school was definitely 'work', separated from any personal purpose, but done to demonstrate to the teacher that learning was taking place. The second point concerns the wide variation in children's perceptions about what writing means.

In a similar survey carried out in Sheffield the teachers first of all noted their own purposes for asking the children to write, then asked the children for their views of what the writing was for.[4] Among the teachers' reasons were:

- confidence-building
- to help recall
- building sentences
- to enable them to write creatively

- to gather, record and pass on information
- to aid fluency in reading and writing
- comprehension
- handwriting
- to think logically/to encourage reasoning.

The children thought that they were writing because:

- it's good for me
- it helps us
- it's easy
- we practise words
- we're learning about Indians (work on North America)
- we learn handwriting
- so she knows what I've been doing
- so that the teacher knows how I am doing with my spelling
- we learn about God and animals
- I don't know
- she can mark it.

These examples are not meant to shock or horrify, nor to suggest that teachers are not doing their jobs properly. Far from it. These children's responses showed that they felt that writing was good for them, but that they had not understood their teachers' intentions and had to resort to general comments about why the writing tasks had been set. The teachers who asked the questions were taking their responsibilities very seriously and used the children's comments as the basis for looking carefully and critically at their own approaches to writing in the classroom. Nor does this evidence pretend to come from a statistically accurate sample. Finding out children's perceptions about writing does not need any sophisticated sampling techniques for it to yield useful information for teachers. What these teachers wanted, and got, was evidence from the children they worked with daily, so that they could find ways of making classroom writing more purposeful, more realistic and more likely to allow the children to satisfy some of their own intentions in writing; to bring classroom reasons for writing closer to the everyday home experience of literacy.

These teachers investigated writing in their classrooms before the National Curriculum was introduced. They used their own questions about writing to begin looking at how they could help children develop their capabilities in writing and learning. The National Curriculum for English specifies that a growing ability to write for varying purposes and audiences indicates progress. Even if these areas had not been identified as significant and made part of legislation they would have been included here, since evidence from teachers and researchers has highlighted just how important these factors are in promoting confidence and competence in writing.

Pamela Peters, investigating the writing required of first-year undergraduates at Macquarie University, points to the difficulties experienced by writers who, because they have reached university, can certainly be considered 'successful'. The main problem is that they often find themselves having to write for a distant audience:

> the task of creating an audience must be one of the demands of student composition. It undoubtedly poses a problem for inexperienced writers, who are not used to constructing a consistent audience profile and may do so erratically.[5]

Much younger writers can undoubtedly benefit from having some idea of who will read their writing, as Margaret Wallen explains:

> When children perceive there is a readership for their writing beyond that offered by their teacher, their motivation and enthusiasm increase enormously. This gives them the impetus to sustain effort through several drafts and gives the teacher an unquestionable justification for demanding technical accuracy and good presentation.[6]

The evidence is already clear, and many teachers have discovered for themselves just how much progress children can make when they have clearer perceptions about why they are writing. But this is not the end of the story. Many teachers have experienced the roller-coaster feeling of great excitement when an activity which uses writing has allowed children to achieve more than might have been expected, only to be followed by a sense of anti-climax when the pressing needs of daily classroom life mean a return to less active and involved tasks. The real challenge lies not in finding that exciting activity in the first place, but in working out how the achievements and insights which came from it can be embedded in everyday practice. Even more challenging is to manage to keep pace with monitoring progress, assessing it and planning for future achievement.

Describing progress

If writing is to be recognized as an important means of learning in all areas of the curriculum then any adequate or useful description of development will need to take account of a range of factors. Most particularly, it will need to cover progress over a period of time and to include comments about writing behaviour – choices of forms of writing; readiness to redraft where necessary; awareness of when writing can be discarded when it has done its job. Since it is clear that children's achievements are dependent on the opportunities and challenges they have been offered, a full description will require some account of context. This can form a useful record, not only for the class teacher but for teachers in other classes or schools, or for parents. ILEA's *Primary Language Record* offers a helpful framework for a form of recording which can capture both the process and the tangible evidence of progress, rather than relying on more traditional forms of record-keeping which yield little useful information.[7]

However, in practice, the carefully documented approach to the *Primary*

Language Record means a significant amount of work by teachers and the intentions behind such record-keeping can so easily founder on the rocks of teacher overload. The danger is that the descriptive accounts which promise to be so informative to other teachers will degenerate into those formulaic clichés and euphemisms that are so familiar simply because teachers do not have time to consider precisely what they want to say about a child's language capabilities, or because the carefully constructed record is so full that it proves too much for a receiving teacher to read and take in about a whole class. Lack of time may well mean that records like the *Primary Language Record* model end up doing the opposite of what they were designed to do. This has been the fate of so many enlightened initiatives which cannot be supported by equally enlightened time allocation. But there is another important aspect of compiling records of children's progress in writing which is central to making a genuinely informative description available – that of deciding what to describe and, more importantly, how to describe it. When faced with the writing produced by a whole class over a whole year, just how does a teacher decide what to include as significant and what to leave out? And when looking at a child's writing, what features, apart from spelling and punctuation, are important? Teachers know that there is more to writing development than accuracy in surface technicalities, but how best to describe these features is another matter.

One difficulty lies in the knowledge that, no matter what may be said or written by people with little or no classroom experience, development does not follow a straight upward path. As we learn anything, and get better at it by practice, we all suffer reversals and plateaux. There are times when nothing seems to be happening, and then ability shows itself by sudden spurts of confidence. A technique learned in one context can be revisited and improved in another. In other words, development follows a looping, recursive pattern. And writing development is no different, which makes it difficult to pin down descriptions of progress in any simple way. It is certainly not enough, as many teachers have stressed, to make statements about progress based on single tests, or on checklists of individual 'skills' which have apparently been accomplished – or, more damaging to children's real progress – apparently have not!

The need for careful and considered teacher assessments of individual progress has recently become even more important because of the potential impact such assessments may have on children's futures. The Department of Education and Science's own Task Group on Assessment and Testing makes this explicit in its advice to schools:

> Teachers can make assessments over a longer period and in a greater variety of ways than any external system can provide, and they know the many individual characteristics that affect each pupil's response to tests. . . . Teachers will have to deal with a wide range of knowledge and be able to encourage pupils to show a wide variety of skills and abilities.[8]

Teachers need to establish clear and focused ways of describing progress and these will require concise formats if they are to give genuinely considered information which has not had to be compiled in a hurry by already fatigued teachers. This is important not only to preserve the teachers themselves, but also to ensure a proper evaluation which, in contrast to earlier forms of assessment, is to 'go public'. The implications for individual children and for the schools themselves are as yet rather unclear, but certainly such public availability of evaluations and assessments will be critical for many. Writing remains the major means of making assessments on children's progress and for this reason it is important to establish a concise and informative way for teachers to make their own assessments.

One effective way of demonstrating progress can be to keep examples of children's writing over a period of time. But simply keeping writing samples is not enough. There needs to be some kind of evaluation of writing, some analysis of just what counts as progress, both for internal assessment and as a means of helping children identify indicators of their own progress and areas they need to work on. Teachers' own observations, as well as the requirements of the National Curriculum in England and Wales, indicate two significant areas which should be included in any adequate description of development.

The first is children's growing ability to use writing to say what they want to say, or do what they want it to do. When children begin to make choices about the kinds of writing which will fulfil their own purposes or intentions, then they are showing evidence of having understood that writing is a means of expression which has some significance for them. More than this, they are showing that they understand that they have some control over writing. Taken as indicators of progress, these choices and intentions can be observed in children from the moment they enter school. After experiencing a wide variety of opportunities for writing, the possibilities for progress increase.

The second is children's increasing awareness that someone is going to read any writing which is done – it may be the writer or it may be someone else. Depending on who the reader is likely to be, the writer will increasingly take account of what that reader needs to know in order to make sense of what is written. Shaping writing to take account of the needs of a reader marks an equally significant area of development comparable with the capacity to shape writing to fulfil the writer's own needs. A child who feels strongly about an issue might make a conscious choice between writing an entry in a journal or a letter in order to express her opinions, but having made that choice she will need to make some further decisions depending on who will be reading what she has written. The journal entry may go no further than herself, her friends or her teacher, in which case she can depend on some degree of shared knowledge as she outlines her ideas and feelings; a letter to someone outside the classroom will need a greater amount of explicit detail about the particular issue if it is to do the job she wants it to do.

The National Curriculum for English expresses these areas of progress as 'a growing ability to construct and convey meaning in written language, matching style to purpose and audience.' The Statements of Attainment give details. At Level 3, children should

> begin to revise and redraft in discussion with the teacher, other adults, or other children in the class, paying attention to meaning and clarity as well as checking for matters such as correct and consistent use of tenses and pronouns.[9]

At Level 4, they should be able to

> produce, independently, pieces of writing showing evidence of a developing ability to structure what is written in ways that make the meaning clear to the reader; demonstrate in their writing generally accurate use of sentence punctuation.

and

> ... organise non-chronological writing for different purposes in orderly ways.[10]

At Level 5 they are called upon to

> write in a variety of forms for a range of purposes and audiences, in ways which attempt to engage the interest of the reader.[11]

At Level 6 they should be writing

> in a variety of forms for a range of purposes presenting subject matter differently to suit the needs of specified known audiences and demonstrating the ability to sustain the interest of the reader.[12]

And at Level 9 the aim is that they should be able to

> produce a sustained piece of writing when the task demands it.[13]

But anyone who has worked with very young children will know that, given the right opportunities, they can achieve what is described at Level 6 and beyond and shape writing for 'specified known audiences'; also, that quite inexperienced writers can produce sustained pieces of writing when they are keen to make their meanings clear to others, although this is considered to be a feature of much more mature writers' performance. On the other hand, experienced writers can have difficulties in 'organising non-chronological writing ... in an orderly way' while this is described as an element of the much earlier Level 4. This is not simply to snipe at the National Curriculum in England and Wales, since these extracts need to be looked at as part of the whole range of Statements of Attainment for Writing, but to indicate the complexity of describing development in writing and to suggest that teachers need a rather more helpful way of analysing progress than the Statements alone provide.

If teachers make judgements about progress based only on the descriptions provided in the Statements of Attainment, or feel that they have to teach towards the Levels as described, the children's progress could be threatened. There needs to be some way of looking at children's writing which will help teachers describe this 'growing ability' more precisely. The analytical framework described in Chapter 2 is intended as a basis for looking in a clearer and more focused way at children's writing. Part of this analysis takes into account the writer's intentions – what the writer wants to say – and the ways in which the writer has taken into account the needs of the reader. But there is more to development in writing than the two areas already outlined. Put crudely, the ability to adapt writing to fit specific demands of purpose and audience are the 'what' of writing. Some attention has to be paid to 'how'. How children construct written texts involves looking at organisation and technical competence. This is not an unfamiliar requirement. For many years teachers have used these aspects as indicators of progress. But it is important to recognize that over-emphasis on technical features, the 'how' of writing, can be disabling to young writers and learners. Many children have been led to believe that technical accuracy, rather than the meaning conveyed by the words, is the most important element of writing and many have found writing painful and difficult because of an emphasis on technical accuracy alone. Even today you don't have to go far to find children who have 'wrist lock' when faced with wanting to write a word they don't feel confident to spell, or whose dependence on rubbing out words which are spelled in an unorthodox way prevents them from getting their meanings down on paper.

There are two very serious points about fear impeding children's progress. One is that it is crucial that they are given help both to write what they want to write and to make the finished piece as accurate as they can. Teachers want to help children get it right. Encouraging children to take risks and to experiment with unfamiliar words so that they can explore ideas does not imply a total rejection of achieving technical accuracy. The second point is that if we do not help children overcome a fear of writing, then we will prevent them from using their full potential for learning in all areas of the curriculum – not just in language work. Not only is writing an important tool for constructing, clarifying and working through ideas, and so crucial in the process of learning, it remains the major part of evidence that learning has, in fact, taken place. Since children are to be assessed in all areas of the curriculum, a fear of writing or an unwillingness to explore ideas through writing will have an impact on all their learning.

There are, of course, no magic tricks which can transform fearful writers overnight into confident and fluent writers and learners. Those teachers who have managed to encourage confidence and competence explain that it depends on a steady and planned approach. One of the major factors has been to help children understand that writing is a way of capturing first thoughts as well as an important means of communication, and to help them to find ways of revising and editing writing when accuracy matters. Providing opportunities for children to write for different purposes and readers is the first step towards helping them deal with matters of organization and technical accuracy.

Two further elements in any useful description of development in writing, then, are those which consider the way texts are put together, and those which deal with technical features of syntax, vocabulary, punctuation and spelling. As writers become more aware of what they want to write and who might be reading their writing, they will need to develop their knowledge of possible forms for writing and to increase their ability to select particular sentence structures, vocabulary and punctuation to suit their intentions in writing. They need, in other words, some notion of genre, of the patterned forms of writing which have been developed within our society to carry particular kinds of messages. In developing their awareness of and their capabilities of using different genres for writing children are not only learning how to organize writing, but also extending their experience of different ways of thinking about texts. Bruner's elegantly simple definition expresses what an understanding of genre can offer both to a writer and to a reader of different kinds of texts: Genre seems to be a way of both organizing the structure of events and organizing the telling of them.[14] In his definition, genre is not only about categories which can be used to describe different forms and purposes of writing, but a way of helping a learner make sense of experience. Genre encompasses, then, both the process of putting texts together to make meaning and the final form in which that process finds expression. For teachers, coming to understand genre as a way of organizing thought as well as of describing texts, is essential if children are genuinely to be able to use writing to form and communicate their thoughts. And if writing is to communicate effectively, developing writers will, finally, need to be able to proof-read, or ask for help in proof-reading, if the writing is to 'go public'. What can be done, then, to help children develop competence in both the organization and the technical accuracy of texts?

Building up knowledge about language

There has been some anxiety about the areas of the National Curriculum for English which deal with knowledge about language. Does it signal a return to teaching technical terminology or grammatical points out of context? Will this requirement need particular expertise which teachers fear they do not have? Not necessarily. The ability to deal effectively with knowledge about language without stultifying children's efforts or spending time on pointless exercises will depend to a great extent on teachers being able to identify the knowledge which children are using to make meaning and to find ways of making that knowledge an explicit and everyday part of talking about language. When children's existing knowledge is identified, the teacher is in a strong position to extend that knowledge. At the risk of seeming to go round in circles, the most effective means of helping children to extend their knowledge about forms and genres of writing and how technical features can best be deployed in particular writing tasks, is to plan for a varied range of writing experiences which are based on an understanding of the need for acknowledged purposes and a recognized readership – and then to talk about them. With this kind of firm base, the aspects of the National Curriculum which deal with knowledge about language begin to look less daunting.

In a discussion of knowledge about language, John Richmond asserts that: 'The most important kind of knowledge about language is implicit knowledge'.

He stresses the importance of the context for language use in helping to make this implicit knowledge explicit:

> The most important job for the adults who care for the child is to help the child's implicit knowledge develop. For teachers, this means providing a classroom environment which supports and affirms the child's achievements, while continually proposing activities calling forth greater powers of articulation and understanding. The essential business of the language and English curriculum is, in fact, to provide opportunities for pupils to compose, communicate and comprehend meanings, their own and other people's, in purposeful contexts. Within these contexts, pupils' competence as users of language develops.[15]

Often, children's writing shows their considerable competence as language users – their versatility in putting texts together. They can use varying sentence structures and punctuate according to the effects they want to achieve. These capabilities will have become part of their knowledge of texts built up over time, from their own reading, by being introduced to examples of different forms of writing and by learning strategies for revising and editing their own work. Looking at children's written texts can give some useful clues about their implicit knowledge about language. Part of the job of helping children to develop as writers is to find ways in which they can bring this implicit knowledge to the surface, be able to talk about their writing and recognize just how they have put texts together for particular purposes. This may well depend upon the teacher's confidence in recognizing their own knowledge about language. John Richmond points out that:

> Teachers, like pupils, already have much valuable knowledge about language derived from their experience as human beings in the world. There is no hard line dividing teachers' 'human' knowledge from their 'professional' knowledge, any more than it is possible to divide pupils' classroom language development from their experience of language in the world.[16]

It is essential, then, for teachers to find ways of recognizing and affirming what they themselves know about language if they are to help children extend and develop their language use. One way for teachers to begin would be to consider how to create contexts for discussion about writing; about different kinds of writing to do different jobs; about how writing and talking interact, differ and converge, and to introduce opportunities for experiment in purposeful contexts.

In the Writing component of the National Curriculum for English, for example, it is required that children should be able at Level 4 to

> begin to use the structures of written Standard English and begin to use some sentence structures different from those of speech.

as well as to

> ... discuss the organisation of their own writing; revise and redraft the writing as appropriate, independently, in the light of that discussion.[17]

and at Level 5 to

show in discussion the ability to recognise variations in vocabulary according to purpose, topic and audience and according to whether language is spoken or written.[18]

Just how can a teacher create opportunities for these kinds of discussion? What kinds of activity will help children make explicit what they already know about language and create further opportunities for them to learn new ways of talking about the structures and purposes of writing?

After a visit to a shipyard, this 7-year-old wrote, as a fourth draft after discussion with the teacher and others in the classroom, the following:

> When we were at home we looked at some leaflets and I spotted the HMS Warrior and I asked granny if we could go to it and she said yes so we packed a picnic and set off We got to the HMS Warrior and it was very hot and there were a lot of people. there were signs to show us around and I was very excited. The anckor was on boad so the ship would not tilt sideways.

There are several examples here of this young writer's 'growing ability to use structures different from those of speech', as well as evidence of his oral language feeding into his writing.

His written comments on the process of putting his text together help us to see the extent of his knowledge about how he can make language work for him:

> After brainstorming I shared with Sebastian. He wrote down 4 questions for me. They helped because I had to get more information down to answer them and they came up in the writing. I was Amazed how well his questions did. 2 and 3 were the hardest to Answer. 4 really got me thinking about an answer.
>
> I did my piece of writing and I was pleased with it and That I was Able to Answer the questions. I shared it with Mrs fawcett. She cut the first bit up and asked me to try it in a different order. so I read it out to everbody two different ways. They liked the second way and then I did it a third way and they liked that best. I wanted to keep in one bit but when I read it out loud I realized it didn't fit.
>
> I read all my writing through and then look at my brainstorm again. I found boilers and pulleys and decied to write about those.[19]

This writer is clearly able to talk about variations in vocabulary and organization 'according to purpose, topic and audience'.

It might be an interesting activity for teachers to take these extracts and consider just what kinds of knowledge about language this young writer is demonstrating he has. He certainly shows remarkable competence. But the most interesting point of conjecture is to do with what the teacher had done to make it possible for him to articulate his knowledge. In line with John Richmond's comments, this teacher has provided a context in which all the pupils can develop their implicit knowledge about language. Part of this context forms the second element of his outline of how teachers' knowledge about language should be made part of classroom experience: 'their *interventions* in language use with pupils in order to give advice . . . suggest lines of further development'.[20] While it may not be possible for teachers to find occasions when they can have detailed conversations with all children about how they can use language to fulfil their own purposes, it is possible to encourage children to talk to each other about writing so that they learn how to become more careful and critical readers of their own writing. One final extract shows just how this can work:

> When I was Emma's response partner I read her writing to her so that she could hear what she had actually written. when people do that for me I find it helpful. you can discuss things with them. I thought it was too long an I suggested that she cut more out. She had a quick think and agreed with me. we disagreed once and Emma made the decision because it was her writing.[21]

These children have discovered not just that they can talk together about writing to improve it, but have come to understand something important about the whole process of learning. One 'finds it helpful' to talk things over; the other 'had a quick think'; together they negotiated ways of reaching decisions. The different kinds of partnerships – between the children, between children and teachers, or between children and other adults – which contribute to the making of a text like this, demonstrate the value of such discussions. They allow reflection on writing, a chance to try it out on others, to stand back and see if it is, in fact, doing the job the writer wanted it to do. The same chances for reflections through partnerships and dialogues are made when teachers explain the working of language to children. In John Richmond's words: 'Teachers' knowledge about language is, in fact, their working theory of language in learning.'[22] Talking with pupils about how language is put together and how it can be changed to make specific and chosen meanings, is part of a language policy in action – a policy which recognizes that language is both social and individual, part of the mixing of cultures which everyone, including the teacher, brings to the classroom. It is a starting point for a much broader understanding about how writing contributes to learning and how the context for learning is a critical factor in children's success or failure. There is no doubt that children gain from talking about writing and coming to understand that their writing will be read by others for the meaning it conveys; that writing need not just be a routine exercise marked by the teacher and returned for correction. When they perceive writing as a way of fulfilling their own intentions to communicate, children are well on the way to knowing that they are, in fact, writers. But that understanding needs to become a useful and lasting foundation for future progress. It needs both a wider and a deeper perception of what writing is or can be.

The wider view

Probably because of the traditional view of writing as a finished product, a great deal of writing which goes on in classrooms becomes 'invisible'. It's not uncommon to visit a classroom where the teacher says 'They haven't done any writing today' when quite clearly the children have been using writing for all sorts of reasons. They may have been recording data while doing some maths or technology investigations; brainstorming ideas for a history project; making notes to report back on discussions; taking a little time to write in journals; writing comments about particularly enjoyable books they have read; writing notes to each other; doing wordsearches, crosswords or playing word games to use time profitably. What we all understand from the teacher's comment is that the children have not been asked to do any 'formal' or extended writing. If children are to understand in a wider way the uses that writing can have for them, there needs to be a recognition of the value of all kinds of writing – not just the more public or extended pieces which are seen to express personal or imaginative ideas. Writing needs to be seen not just as part of a process towards a finished product, but also as a way of working. Those 'invisible' uses of writing – the notes we make to help us sort out ideas, the plans, the jottings which remind us of what we have done or need to do – all have relevance or importance in moving our ideas forward. Our own record books, diaries, journals, memos, notes taken from meetings – which are often seen by no one else but ourselves – similarly serve an important purpose in helping us capture, clarify and reflect on our thoughts. The notes we make to help us chair meetings, take assembly, talk with parents – writing which leads towards a spoken outcome – give us a framework for sorting out ideas, for making sure that we say what we want to say. Letters to friends or members of the family, postcards, birthday greetings – none of which will be redrafted before they are sent – fulfil personal and satisfying purposes for us and allow us to express emotions, concerns and cares which not only communicate our feelings but often make us feel better because we have shared part of our social lives with others without having to be overconcerned with formal technicalities; in fact, we often experiment with technical devices of punctuation and syntax when we write to friends or family. We can use more, and more varied, punctuation and sentence structure in our enthusiasm to make our voices 'speak off the page'. We can see children using all of these important kinds of writing daily in the classroom, yet they are not always given recognition for the value they have in learning.

However, it is not easy to change children's perceptions of writing and it certainly will not happen overnight. All learning takes time and support. Children will need to have their attention drawn explicitly to the ways in which writing can serve wider purposes. They need to be reminded that the brainstorming they did last week for a science project can be a useful strategy for beginning work in topic or for starting a poem. They need frameworks to help record their changing ideas as they experiment in making a load-bearing bridge in technology. And often these frameworks need only be a series of boxes with lead questions like 'What were your first ideas?' Which did you try out? What did you decide to change? Why? What was the result?' To help make notes from books or other resource material they may need a guide sheet which asks them to find 'key' words; to jot down words which they do not fully understand; to make comparisons between pieces of information taken from different sources; to record page numbers with relevant or important facts or to jot down the title and author of a book used for reference. Children need models and examples of possible ways to use writing to help them work out ideas, capture fleeting thoughts or reflections, analyse and evaluate what they have been doing.[23] Furthermore, for a while they will need reminding that they have used particular strategies before and may like to try using them again; they will need to develop not just confidence with the techniques but also a vocabulary through which they can begin to talk about writing in all its forms. All of these matters have implications for the teacher's role, for the interventions which a teacher makes in helping children to shift their perceptions towards a wider view of writing.

Going deeper

Once children begin to understand that writing can have different uses for them, they are on the way to being able to develop the range of purposes suggested in the National Curriculum in England and Wales as a strong indicator of progress. When they can begin to distinguish between those kinds of writing which do need to be worked on and perfected and those which do not, they are moving towards developing ideas about what writing can do for them. When they begin to understand that they write differently for their personal purposes, for their family or friends and for people they do not know, they have reached a crucial stage in recognizing a range of possible readers of writing. But, once again, it does not stop there. If children are genuinely to take on responsibility for making choices about when it will be useful to write in a particular way for a particular readership – themselves, friends, teachers, others outside the classroom – they will begin to dig deeper into their understanding of writing and how they can use it to fulfil their own purposes or intentions. They will need to be helped to identify just how they have used writing in the past for specific purposes and what they did to make the writing successful. They will need further models and examples and to be given the means to become readers of their own writing just as they read printed text written by others and appearing in books, newspapers and magazines, leaflets, posters, and so on. To be able to develop as writers, then, children need to make their implicit knowledge about writing explicit. They need to pay conscious attention to what they have previously been able to achieve in writing so that they will know how to do it again, or improve on earlier achievements. They cannot do this alone.

One of the unnerving things that happens when children begin to write for a greater range of purposes and a wider readership is that the teacher's role shifts. Sometimes it can seem as though there is a loss of control, or at least of direction, as the work which children are engaged in appears to take on a momentum of its own. When this happens, teachers are often tempted to say: 'I didn't do anything, the children just did it on their own.' But they could not be more wrong! What has happened is that the role has shifted from an overtly directing one towards a much more subtly demanding organizational and consultative position. The major effect has gone into planning the activity, making decisions about when and how it will be best to provide support, response or further challenges, keeping the end point in view and creating the conditions for reaching whatever outcome is wanted. And this need not always be a written product, of course. Helping children plan and script a play is just as much a chance for them to develop writing as it is for them to gain experience of different kinds of oral language. But the most crucial part of the teacher's role as a planner and collaborator is what happens after the work has been completed.

To help children dig deeper into their language resources, to uncover the nuggets of knowledge they hold beneath the surface of conscious awareness, planning needs to be extended to include opportunities for children to evaluate and appreciate what they have achieved through and in writing. As Jerome Bruner suggests, they need an opportunity to take stock and recognize what they can do: 'Much of the process of education consists of being able to distance oneself in some way from what one knows by being able to reflect on one's knowledge.'[24]

Teachers need these kinds of opportunity for reflection, too. Both the detailed analysis of texts and the broader picture of a writing classroom which form the central section of this book are intended to offer a basis for reflection and comparison. Since knowledge about language is important for both teachers and pupils, the framework for looking at writing should help create a greater awareness of elements of text organization. This will, in turn, help provide a context in which children can become more aware of how texts can best be put together to fulfil their own intentions as writers and readers.

The process of becoming an attentive reader of your own writing, of being able to stand back and see what you can do, is, of course, a gradual one. It will depend upon the opportunities offered in the classroom and the teacher's own view of what counts as 'successful' writing. In the early years, children do not evolve as writers only by being given chances to write.[25] This is the essential first step in setting up positive expectations of themselves as writers, but it is not enough on its own. They make most progress when they are given varied contexts for writing – the 'home' corner; play; the writing table – combined with teachers' responses to the writing and sensitive interventions to draw attention to what they have written. There is always structure and guidance, even though this may not be in the older tradition of all children being given formal instruction at the same time, or of using just one approach to sentence-making. For effective learning to take place we all need opportunities to try things out, to make mistakes and to learn from them with guidance. When children have gained confidence with the technicalities of forming letters, words, sentences, and longer pieces of text, they similarly need opportunities to learn how to make their writing more effective. Some of these can be found at the very personal level of 'Were these notes useful to me?'; some need to be tested out by other people's response to the question 'Does this make sense?'. But no teacher is going to be able to respond carefully and conscientiously to all the writing which children produce and this is one sound practical reason why encouraging collaboration over writing is an effective way to promote children's development as writers.[26]

Partnerships for writing

But there is an equally sound theoretical reason why children should have opportunities for collaborating over writing. Bruner's description of the need to be able to take stock of what we know is enlarged by his view that learning necessarily involves sharing developing ideas:

> I have come increasingly to recognise that most learning in most settings is a communal activity, a sharing of the culture. It is not just that the child must make his knowledge his own, but that he must make it his own in a community of those who share his sense of belonging to a culture.[27]

This emphasis on a shared culture leads to a clearer definition of just what collaboration over writing might mean. It need not mean a group or pair of children working together on the same text. It can mean a whole variety of different ways in which children, parents, teachers and other members of a community can work together. In *Collaboration and Writing* Morag Styles points out the importance of John Richmond's definition of the classroom as 'a community of writers'. The accounts of collaborative writing which she introduces include:

> teachers writing alongside pupils, parents and other members of the community drawn into writing ventures, pupils' writing published and read by a real audience; and, of course, all sorts of ways and means of pupils writing with and for each other.[28]

In considering just what the teacher's role might be in such collaborative activities perhaps a more precise description would be 'partnership'. Partners do not always do the same things at the same time – their efforts are shared. Similarly, fruitful partnerships depend upon using the strengths of each partner to best effect. Teachers' partnerships with children for writing may mean that the child initiates the reason for writing and the teacher gives advice or guidance; or that the teacher provides the starting point or models a way of writing which the children can then try out for themselves. There are no hard and fast rules about how such partnerships should be carried out. They evolve as the partners discover each other's strengths. But because the teacher has experience of how to help children learn, and so has a longer-term view of what might be possible, the planning for progress starts with the teacher who gradually encourages the less experienced partners to take more responsibility for their own writing. This is not to suggest, however, that decisions about the content of the curriculum or about the progress of learning should pass out of the hands of the teacher. Far from it. Encouraging children to take on greater partnership responsibility for writing does not mean that they should be expected to make judgements which they are not experienced enough to make. It means that the teacher makes plans based on observations of the children's growing capabilities and these will always be made from the point of view of someone who has expertise in organizing for learning.

There should be no confusion here about power and responsibility. Many enlightened ideas in education have foundered or been misunderstood because, in a rush of enthusiasm, the baby has been thrown out with the bathwater. The idea that children are capable of taking greater power and responsibility for the development of their own writing capabilities does not mean that they should be seen as greater experts than their teachers. This would be massively unfair to children. What is very clear, however, is that partnership can promote effective progress. As Vygotsky points out, for many years we have judged children's progress in learning by past – and, significantly, individual – achievements alone, although this tells us little about how their learning might develop in the future. A more informative way of looking at progress is to see what children can do when they have support:

> In studies of children's mental development it is generally assumed that only those things that children can do on their own are indicative of mental abilities. We give children a battery of tests or a variety of tasks of varying degrees of difficulty, and we judge the extent of their mental development on the basis of how they solve them and at what level of difficulty. On the other hand, if we offer leading questions or show how the problem is to be solved and the child then solves it, or if the teacher initiates the solution and the child completes it or solves it in collaboration with other children – in short, if the child barely misses an independent solution of the problem – the solution is not regarded as indicative of mental development. . . . even the profoundest thinkers never questioned the assumption; they never entertained the notion that what children can do with the assistance of others might be in some sense even more indicative of their mental development than what they can do alone.[29]

Encouraging children to collaborate over writing puts principles into action. It recognizes that children have potential for participating in their own learning; that writing is valuable for the part it plays in working out ideas as well as making for genuine communication. In *Common Knowledge*, Derek Edwards and Neil Mercer explore the development of understanding in the classroom. For them Vygotsky offers 'a theory of intellectual development which acknowledged that children undergo quite profound changes in their understanding by engaging in joint activity and conversation with other people'.[30] Language is the fulcrum for these changes: 'First, it provides a medium for teaching and learning. Second, it is one of the materials from which the child constructs a way of thinking.'[31] Partnerships in writing provide more than useful audiences, readers or responders. They are crucial in promoting children's capabilities as learners across the whole range of activities and curriculum areas. Bruner's notion of *handover* is helpful in describing the difficulty of reconciling the twin roles of 'teacher as partner' and 'teacher as leader': 'The essence of the process is that learners do not remain for ever propped up by the scaffold of adult assistance, but come to take control of the process for themselves.'[32]

It is through the planned interventions of teachers who have thought through their classroom practice that this handover can be most effectively carried out. It is not an easy process and both teachers and pupils need to learn when and how to work in partnership and when to offer and take up individual challenges. Much will depend upon the teacher's sensitivity, built up from experience. Developing writers need to have their writing read by others and to read their own writing attentively; they need opportunities to collaborate and to work on individual tasks. Part of the assessment which will help judge the effectiveness of handover in partnerships will be related to how far young writers have learned to use writing in different ways and to choose specific ways of writing to fit their own purposes and intentions in learning and communicating. Establishing both the collaborative practices which build towards this confidence and a way of evaluating and describing progress is part of the teacher's policy about writing. This kind of policy is founded not only on assessing the merits of finished pieces of writing but also on recognizing progress which is evident in writing behaviour, in the confidence with which young writers tackle tasks and the choices they make about when and how to write in particular ways.

But this is not the end of it. If, following Bruner's suggestions, teachers and children are to be able to stand back and notice progress so that learning can be affirmed and consolidated, and if the classroom is to be seen as a place of communal endeavour creating a shared culture, two more moves have to be made. One is for the teacher to find ways of describing progress which reflect the achievements evident in the process of learning as well as in any finished pieces of writing which can be taken as tangible evidence of progress. The second is to find ways of sharing such descriptions with the children so that they can take a more active part in recognizing and using their own growing knowledge about their writing capabilities.

Evaluation and assessment

This is where partnerships for writing make their greatest impact. When children begin to evaluate their own writing they become more aware of the kinds of criteria which can be used to judge effectiveness. Their teachers will have the chance to explain why certain aspects of their writing need attention, and teacher and child can begin to plan together ways of making writing more effective.

In her book *When Writers Read*, Jane Hansen explains her views about children being involved in evaluation. Working in New Hampshire with children aged 6 and 7, she asked the following questions:

- What's something new you've learned to do with writing?
- What would you like to learn so that you can become a better writer?

She then tells about one child's response:

> Karey, a first-grade girl, in regard to what she's recently learned in writing said, 'I think.'

I asked her to explain and she said, 'I think about what to write about. I look around the room and think about what each person has written. Andrea, Vanessa and Sarah have all written about rainbows so I decided to, but mine's different. One day Carolyn wrote: "I SAW A WATER FOUNTAIN. IT WAS PRETTY." I decided to write about a water fountain I saw, and wrote what Carolyn wrote but then did the rest myself.'

Jane Hansen comments:

> These children often talk about what they do when they write and are beginning to talk about what they do when they read. When the processes are familiar to them, this awareness helps them try new options they hear about from friends and teacher. Their own evaluation of their work is the most important aspect of evaluation, because when students know what they do well and choose what they want to work on for growth, their own progress is their goal. Since the root word of *evaluation* is value, the evaluation scheme should reflect whether students value the process of reading itself.[33]

Her remarks apply equally to writing. Evaluation does more than one job. It works for teacher and children, showing just what is valued and valuable about any piece of writing, and helps build towards a continuing record of what any child can do with writing. As part of the long-term planning for developing writing, it gives indications of where to go next.

At the same time as encouraging children to become attentive readers and evaluators of their own work, teachers will be involved in a rather different kind of evaluation and assessment. With knowledge of the longer-term aims for what they want children to learn, and the experience of seeing a great deal of children's writing over some time, teachers will be able to set their assessments in a wider, more informed context. While the children focus on shorter-term aims, teachers will be aware of what is possible during a term or a year – the ground they want to cover – as well as taking account of the kinds of assessment which will be needed for the National Curriculum. There is no doubt that these are heavy responsibilities which threaten to become intolerable burdens to both teachers and children if the need for assessment takes greater prominence than the desire to provide a varied and stimulating curriculum which involves writing in all its forms.

Assessing just how children are developing as writers and learners will mean paying attention to:

1 purposes for writing and the ways in which children make their written intentions clear;
2 providing opportunities for children to write for varied audiences and to recognize the differences in the ways they write according to who is going to read the writing;
3 the organization of texts and ways of introducing models and strategies for different forms of writing;

4 talking about technical features and finding ways of helping children recognize and extend their knowledge about language.

Putting these different elements into action becomes a policy for developing writing and learning. It is founded on principles which acknowledge: the language resources which children bring to school, and the importance of children's active involvement in expressing and creating their own developing knowledge, supported by the teacher's informed planning, careful intervention and continuing evaluation. The teacher's crucial role will be guided by general principles about how best to organize a supportive and stimulating environment for developing language and learning and some detailed knowledge about writing.

It is a demanding agenda. It requires teachers to feel confident about their own knowledge about written texts – what makes them effective; how to help children increase their versatility in using writing to fulfil their own intentions as well as in being able to use accepted genres for recognized purposes. The next chapter begins to unpick some of the threads which make up the texture of different kinds of writing. In putting some writing under the microscope we are suggesting a way of beginning to make clear just what a description of development in writing might include and how a simple analytical framework can lead to a much fuller appreciation of just what children show they can do as they put together different written texts.

Notes

1 The school where we did our work, Burnham Copse Junior, has few bilingual children. All the children in our sample used English as their mother tongue. This may suggest that the book cannot offer much to schools where some or many of the children have access to more than one language. It is true that the writing examples we use are not from children who offer this kind of richness in language resources, but it would be a mistake to assume that monolingual experience cannot offer insights into linguistic diversity. As the introduction to Nelson/National Writing Project, *A Rich Resource: Writing and language diversity*, Kingston, Nelson (1990) points out:

> Even those of us who see ourselves as monolingual, using only Standard English, vary our language according to the audience, purpose and context of our communication . . .
> Children, too, can use language in these different ways, and can vary forms and registers appropriately.

One most important principle to keep in mind when considering language diversity, whether in bilingual, multilingual or apparently monolingual communities, is that linguistic identity is closely bound up with children's social, emotional and cultural experience. Recognition of the value of the language communities which go to make up the school community will be a critical factor in establishing a flourishing environment for learning.

2. See Nelson/National Writing Project, *Partnerships for Writing: School, the Community and the Workplace*, Kingston, Nelson (1990).
3. These responses are just a few of the many from children aged between 7 and 11 from Burnham Copse Junior School, Tadley, Hampshire.
4. K. Stallard, *Encouraging Confidence in Writers*, Sheffield, Sheffield Writing at the Transition Project (1988).
5. P. Peters, 'Getting the theme across: a study of the dominant function in the academic writing of university students' in B. Couture (ed.), *Functional Approaches to Writing: Research Perspectives*, London, Frances Pinter (1986).
6. M. Wallen, in Nelson/National Writing Project, *Audiences for Writing*, Kingston, Nelson (1989), p. 8.
7. M. Barrs, *et al.*, *The Primary Language Record*, London, ILEA/CLPE (1988).
8. Department of Education and Science and Welsh Office, *National Curriculum Task Group on Assessment and Testing Report – A digest for schools*, London, HMSO (1988), p. 11.
9. Department of Education and Science, *English in the National Curriculum* (No. 2), London, HMSO (1989), p. 12.
10. Ibid., p. 13.
11. Ibid.
12. Ibid., p. 14.
13. Ibid., p. 15.
14. J. S. Bruner, *Actual Minds: Possible Worlds*, Cambridge, Mass., Harvard Educational Press (1986), p. 6.
15. J. Richmond, 'What do we mean by knowledge about language?' in *The North Circular: the Magazine of the North London Consortium*, London, Language in the National Curriculum Project (1990), p. 5.
16. Ibid., p. 12.
17. Department of Education and Science, *English in the National Curriculum* (No. 2), p. 13.
18. Ibid., p. 13.
19. We are grateful to Alexander Bailey of Rushall School, near Pewsey, Wiltshire, for letting us use these extracts; also to Jo Fawcett, the class teacher, and Gill Clarkson, then Co-ordinator for the 'Write to Learn' Project in Wiltshire, for pointing out to us what Alexander's writing revealed about his knowledge about language.
20. Richmond, 'What do we mean', p. 12, original emphasis.
21. Alexander's writing.
22. Richmond, 'What do we mean', p. 12.
23. See Nelson/National Writing Project, *Responding to and Assessing Writing*, Kingston, Nelson (1989), pp. 29–40.
24. Bruner, *Actual Minds*, p. 127.
25. See, for example, the introduction to Nelson/National Writing Project *Becoming a Writer*, Kingston, Nelson (1989); and J. Hansen, *When Writers Read*, Portsmouth, NH, Mary Glasgow (1988), pp. 5–16.
26. Chapter 5 takes up these points in much greater detail.
27. Bruner, *Actual Minds*, p. 127.
28. M. Styles, (ed.), *Collaboration and Writing*, Milton Keynes, Open University Press (1989), p. 3.

29 L. S. Vygotsky, *Mind in Society*, Cambridge, Mass., Harvard University Press (1987), p. 85.
30 D. Edwards and N. Mercer, *Common Knowledge – the development of understanding in the classroom*, London, Methuen (1987), p. 19.
31 Ibid., p. 20.
32 Ibid., p. 23.
33 Hansen, *When Writers Read*, pp. 89–90.

2 Starting points

As outlined in Chapter 1, trying to describe writing development is a tricky business. For a description to be helpful it needs to be quite detailed. It needs to take into account not only what children's writing shows about their present capabilities, but also what they might be able to do with writing in the future. In Vygotsky's terms it needs not only to be able to describe their actual developmental levels but also to give some clues about their potential or proximal development – what they may be able to do with help. Even that, however, is not enough. The success or otherwise of a piece of writing depends on whether the writer does, in fact, manage to make the writing do what it was intended to do – communicate ideas or facts; amuse or entertain; sort out ideas. Judging the effectiveness of a piece of writing often depends on the response that it receives from the reader. For writers to be able to make their intentions clear in writing, and for readers to be able to give a genuine response, depends on the opportunities offered for the writing to matter, both the writer and the reader. If the purpose is clear and the likely readership is known, writing will be more effective than if children feel they are simply being asked to fulfil a task which is intended only to test what they can (or cannot) show they have achieved. All of these factors will influence a description of writing development, since if the opportunities are not offered, even the most confident writers will have difficulties in showing the best that they can do. To add to the complexity, children's ability to take up the opportunities offered rests to a large extent on their previous experiences of writing.

A description of development, then, needs to reflect past, present and future writing possibilities and place these alongside a knowledge of the opportunities provided for young writers to try their hand in a variety of forms and contexts. In this chapter we start by looking at some examples written by 10- and 11-year-olds who have reached the end of their primary school experience. Starting with the oldest children in the age range gives us a chance to look back as well as forward; to begin to identify some of the features which might be taken as indicators of progress in writing as well as considering how the young writers in our sample are poised for development. The following chapters step back to earlier years, both to consider the classroom context for writing and to begin to trace the steps which young children make as they develop as writers. This leads to suggestions for a form of assessment and evaluation of writing achievement which can build to a simple and effective means of record-keeping.

Despite the complexity of describing development in writing, we had to begin with a framework of some kind. Our working definition is based on the broad outline given in Chapter 1, seeing writing development as reflecting increasing ability to:

1 fulfil the writer's own purposes or intentions and to choose the most suitable way of doing this;
2 take account of the needs of the reader;
3 use different forms, genres or formats for writing;
4 handle technical conventions.

In an attempt to see if these descriptive categories would help us detect features of children's writing which could lead to a useful form of continuing evaluation, we first looked closely at two examples of one child's writing. Although we knew that one of the pieces had been the result of a cross-curricular topic and we were familiar with the teacher and the school, we had little other information about the context for the writing, and none about the writer, Steven.

Looking at writing out of context can pose some problems; there are always questions which the reader wants to ask. However, in analysing these two examples we hoped we might begin to identify areas which, even by reading a text 'cold', can give useful information about a writer's capabilities rather than those areas which can only be informed by a knowledge of the context for writing. We hoped this approach would help us clarify the kinds of information which a teacher might need to know and record if a full description of progress is to be made.

A framework for analysis

One of the decisions we took when setting out our analytical framework was that we would make strenuous attempts only to comment on what was there in the text. This meant trying not to infer capabilities or go beyond the evidence of the texts themselves. This was partly because we wanted to see just what could be drawn from isolated texts before we went on to look at several pieces by one writer; it could be helpful, too, in suggesting to teachers a means of assessing what a child can do *now* in order to begin to build up a framework for evaluation which can look forward to what she can be helped to do in the future.

Our decision also meant looking for positive features in the texts we examined. As outlined earlier, there has been a strong tradition of looking for what writers cannot do. We do not want to suggest that teachers should never look for error. That would be both foolish and ultimately unhelpful to developing writers.

Looking for pattern in error is a very effective way to help children move forward and an issue which we take up later. But since we were starting by looking at isolated pieces of writing just to see what could be identified from them it seemed fruitless to focus on what the writers could *not* do; we needed to find out if a framework like the one we envisaged could give us helpful positive leads on children's capabilities as writers.

Importantly, however, we do not want to suggest that the comments we have made on the selected examples of writing are the only ones that could be made – nor, indeed, that they are necessarily the 'right' ones. We evolved our comments by looking at the texts and discussing what we thought we could see in them. When a group of teachers get together and engage in a similar activity they can come up with a wealth of observations drawn from just one piece of a child's writing. We should like to think that our readers would do just that – find other interesting aspects of the texts, add to our analyses and even disagree with our conclusions!

In creating analytical categories we decided that the four descriptive indicators of progress outlined above could offer some useful ways in. We have simplified them to the following headings:

1 *Intentions*[1]/*choices*: What does the writing reveal about the child's success in fulfilling the task? What choices are made in attempting to do this?
2 *Awareness of reader*: How does the writing indicate an understanding of the needs of a reader? What strategies does the writer use to help the reader?
3 *Form/organization*: What does the writing indicate about the child's ability to present ideas in a clear and coherent way? How does this fit with the demands of the task?
4 *Technical conventions*: What features suggest competence in handling the technicalities of, for example, syntax, punctuation and spelling? How effectively does the writer vary technical features in relation to intention and readership?

Any form of analytical categorization carries its own problems. Because of the complexities involved in putting a text together categories may overlap, seem arbitrary, or run the risk of missing important aspects of a writer's competence. We are aware of these problems but decided that we needed to start somewhere in trying to find a useful way of highlighting aspects of writing which are worthy of attention and which might help teachers develop methods of observing and recording children's writing capabilities. From previous discussions with teacher colleagues from different areas of the country we were confident that these categories represented areas which teachers consider significant.[2]

We began our attempts at analysing some written work by taking examples from Sue Phillips's class of fourth-year juniors. These children were used to working collaboratively; their teacher encouraged writing in a range of different forms springing from all areas of the curriculum. The children whose writing we used were not, for that class, remarkably more competent writers than their friends but, as the examples show, they have reached a significant level of capability in writing. The general writing competence of the class that we were working with meant that we had to use the work of noticeably able writers, but we saw this as an advantage anyway; it can be quite difficult to give constructive advice and challenge to young writers who no longer have any greater difficulty with surface technicalities but who need other more complex kinds of guidance. If we could find a way of analysing, and so perhaps extending, the abilities of already competent writers, this would test the framework as rigorously as possible.

Before we look at some examples of classroom writing, however, we have taken one example from Steven's writing which Sue came across almost by chance and which arose from Steven's own need to communicate something as clearly as he could. On the day he wrote this Steven was unwell but wanted some work to do at home. He wrote a note for his mother explaining how she could find the work that he wanted in his tray in the classroom. Sue was so impressed with these instructions that she saved the note for us to look at.

> Go in, ~~~~ Go to corner with the Book case. Just before it are some trays. Mine is ~~~~ the top and it has my name on. inside get a yellow book with maths on front and a small blue book and a green book inside. The blue book has A day on and the green book has 8 A day on. Bring both Books please.
>
> out side ~~so~~ on the book case are ~~so~~ some folders. some ~~have~~ have got 3 on, 4 on and 5 on. Go to 5 and take out the card inside of the maths Book. look at the top: ~~Book~~ Book 5 section — and page —. go ~~bak~~ back to the folder and take out 5 and the no. on the section from the card. take out the next one card on from mine.

How much difference does context make?

So we started our analysis of text with a piece of writing which certainly had a clear purpose and an identified reader! But one significant feature of the writing was that it had not been done to fulfil a classroom task. We thought that this might be a useful way of looking at what a young writer shows he can do in more than one context for writing by comparing this note with some writing done in class. First of all, using the categories we outlined above, Figure 1 shows what we felt we could tell about Steven's competence as a writer from his note to his mother. This shows Steven as a confident writer who knows that he can use writing to fulfil his own intentions; he has understood exactly how important it is for instructions to be clear and explicit if they are to do the job. This piece is highly geared to the reader's needs, taking account of his mother's lack of context. The altering of the word 'ask' to 'go to' in the first line indicates that he knows what kinds of descriptive detail will help his mother find the work. Even more importantly, he has learned what information to omit and he is economical with information, including no unnecessary details. The writing shows a high level of technical competence, using punctuation which is helpful to the reader and entirely fits the intention for writing.

If Steven can organise his ideas like this when writing for his own purposes, will he show the same capabilities in a different context? The class had been reading and hearing myths and stories from India, linked with their RE work on Hinduism. They had been asked to create a model of a god which would represent a virtue. Steven and Jay worked together on this, then Steven wrote the explanation which was to tell the teacher how they had decided to make their model represent the virtue they had chosen (Figure 2).

Both pieces of Steven's writing are explanatory and so serve as a way of comparing how he can adapt a similar form of writing according to the context, his own intentions and his knowledge of the reader. His sureness in creating a written dialogue with each of his readers shows that he has understood something important about what writing can do for him. By looking carefully at these two short pieces we felt that we had gained some important information about Steven's capabilities and also felt satisfied that a framework like this can draw attention to some interesting aspects of a child's writing. Taken together, the two pieces show that Steven can vary his choice of language; the tone he adopts for particular purposes; the way he organizes the material; the technical strategies he uses to fulfil the different demands of each writing task. He shows an understanding that his writing will be read by others and adjusts the amount of information given and the language he uses accordingly, indicating clearly that he wants to include the reader in what he is writing.

As we suggested earlier, however, there are important aspects which a 'cold' examination of these texts cannot tell us. We found this evidence of 'gaps' a satisfactory outcome of the analysis as it provided support for two of our underlying assumptions. First, it bears out our sense that teachers themselves will

32 WRITING POLICY IN ACTION

Choices/intentions
- gives explicit instructions
- statement and description to help: 'just before it', 'outside on the bookcase', 'some have got 3 on'
- abbreviates sentences; omits words not necessary for his purpose: 'Go to corner', 'with maths on front'

Awareness of reader
- gives exact details of: location, colour, titles, sections . . .
- remembers to say 'please'
- directly addresses his reader: 'go', 'look', 'take out'
- changes original 'ask' to 'go to' so as not to confuse his mother and his teacher!

> Go in, ~~and~~ Go to corner with the Book case. Just before it are some trays. Mine is ~~about~~ the top and it has my name on. inside get a yellow book with maths on front and a small blue book and a green book inside. The blue book has A day on and the green book has 8 A day on. Bring both Books please.
>
> out side ~~on~~ on the book case are ~~sot~~ some folders. some ~~have~~ have got 3 on, 4 on and 5 on. Go to 5 and take out ~~#~~ the card inside of the maths Book. look at the top: ~~Book~~ Book 5 section — and page —. go ~~back~~ back to the folder and take out 5 and the no. on the section from the card. take out the next one card on from mine.

Form/organization
- organizes material logically
- follows the precise route needed to find the books, visualizing exactly what his mother will need to do

Technical features
- uses accurately: commas, colon, dashes, underlining, full stops
- self-corrects for clarity and accuracy
- spells whole piece correctly

Figure 1

STARTING POINTS 33

Choices/intentions
- achieves purpose; explains why they decided to make their model a mixture of animals
- explains choice of 'virtue' clearly
- chooses suitable tone for explanation – informative and straightforward

Awareness of reader
- speaks directly to the reader (teacher/peers/others?)
- gives details in brackets to help the reader understand
- offers the reader a tempting foretaste – 'cunning' – so holding interest
- knows writing can be a dialogue with his teacher

> God's Values
> Our god is the god of ~~imagesten~~ imagernation. It has the head of a rabbit, the nask of a gariffe, the body of a elephant, the arms of a monky, no hands and has legs of a kangaroo. He gives dreams to people at night and thoughts in the day. In one story, Javen (thats his name) gives an old man a ~~time~~ cunning plan to warn off wild ~~commnal~~ anamles and it saved his life.
>
> Have you written the myth about the god Javen and the old man?
> ★ No! we said it is in another story!

Form/organization
- understands how to arrange information clearly and logically: statement in first sentence, physical description in second, qualities of character (virtue) which benefit people, example of how this works in practice (the 'old man' in the promised story)

Technical features
- writes in sentences, varying structure
- uses brackets correctly
- uses repetition for clarity – 'our god is the god of . . .'
- knows how to use a list for explanation
- evidence of rereading and self-editing (erased words)
- makes only 7 spelling errors in 73 words; gets 'elephant' and 'kangaroo' right

Figure 2

be the most informed evaluators of their pupils' progress in writing: they have the knowledge about the background to the writing itself – what has gone before, those earlier experiences which feed a child's present performance – as well as being able to observe all the other writing activities which the child may carry out during the course of a week, a term or a year. Second, it makes it clear that by establishing a way of looking closely at children's writing and using a framework to help focus ideas, a wealth of features emerge which could otherwise go unnoticed.

This is not to suggest that teachers are inattentive to children's work, nor that they should look closely at every piece of writing each child produces. However, occasional detailed reading can draw attention to indicators of progress which, in the everyday process of reading and responding to children's writing, may not be explicitly recognized.[3]

This first analysis left us with several areas that we wanted to investigate. It was clear that we needed more information about the previous experiences which led to Steven's writing. For instance we could not discover from the text alone:

1 What earlier experiences or models of reading led to his capacity to write such clear explanations.
2 How he has developed an ability to choose a form of writing which will fit his intentions.
3 How he came to understand that his writing would be read for its meaning and that it would be responded to rather than simply 'corrected'.
4 Whether specific technical 'errors' (for instance, lack of capitals) are simply transcription omissions during drafting, temporary lapses or points where he needs help.
5 Whether he is equally at ease in writing in other forms.

When we asked Steven's teacher these questions she told us that he has been used to teachers reading and responding to his writing rather than just 'correcting' or 'marking' it for some time.[4] He and his class expect their writing to be read for its meaning and that they will have the chance to revise, edit and to finish a piece if they wish. These insights are important. They suggest that an analysis like this would be even more effective if it formed part of a continuing record of a child's writing, informed by a knowledge of the writer's experiences and the classroom environment which supports writing.

Tracing experiences of literacy

It is difficult to separate the strands which are interwoven to make a piece of writing. As we saw with Steven's work, looking at writing outside the context in which it is produced means that we lack important information. Although in Steven's case we were able to find most of the answers, we still didn't have a clear picture of all the experiences of reading and writing and the responses to them which have fed into his present achievements. We want to stress that these kinds of insight can best be reached by the class teacher, but even then her knowledge will only be part of the whole picture since any writer is influenced by a variety of experiences – home reading, television, conversations with friends and family – many of which are difficult to identify and trace. Previous literacy experience is an important factor in the development of children's writing capabilities and, as we have seen, not easily detectable from a piece of finished writing, although it *is* possible to see some of the effects of these experiences. If we look closely at several pieces of writing by one child we can see how the child adapts writing to fit varying purposes – to communicate with different readers; to organize information in different ways according to purpose; to produce writing which shows evidence of having learned how to use technical conventions – and, at times, by the young writer's explicit reference to other experiences, we can find reflections of the child's experience of reading, conversation or television watching. Some of these experiences have been absorbed simply by everyday exposure to different forms of communication, but much of the opportunity to practise these forms and to develop the ability to adapt writing to fit different purposes depends upon the teacher's planning and intervention.

Knowing that Steven's class teacher provides a wide range of opportunities for her class to practise writing in a variety of forms, we asked her for a broader sample of as many different forms of writing she could find from just two or three other children in the class. We had looked at Steven's explanation and a set of personal instructions to his mother; we then wanted to ask about other forms of writing, including some which were perhaps non-chronological. Could our analytical framework usefully highlight children's ability to write effectively in other forms?

In making her selection, we asked the class teacher to find a range of writing from children who seemed to her to be not noticeably more or less competent writers than the rest of the class. She decided to ask three children if they could let us look at their writing, explained what the selection was for and together they chose a representative sample of the different kinds of writing they had done during the term. It is important to remember, however, that these pieces are not meant to represent all that any of the children could do with writing. In any term's work some pieces will be inaccessible – they may have been put in a class book or displayed on the wall; they may have been sent to someone else, taken home or even lost! In this case, too, the children had a say in the selection of pieces. Their choice may well be different from any choices that a teacher might make. The samples of writing provided by Oliver, Katherine and Zoe which we analyse in this chapter, then, represent a fairly random collection intended only to serve as a means of testing out our framework for analysis to see if it could form the basis for a productive way of identifying what children can do in a range of writing tasks.

The fact that these pieces do not represent a statistically valid sample is, however, a positive advantage since it mirrors the circumstances of the classroom where teachers find themselves having to respond to a variety of writing within a short space of time and to make judgements about what the writing might represent in terms of the progress of any individual. Not only do these judgements have to be made at the time, but they will build to a cumulative record of what each child can do with writing – a history of their literacy experience and achievements.

Selecting writing for assessment

In fulfilling the statutory requirements to provide an internal assessment to set beside the standardized assessments for English in the National Curriculum, teachers will not be able to make a careful analysis of every piece of writing done by every child in the class. There will have to be some selection. Teachers will have to make some decisions about the kinds of writing they want to evaluate in order to make a full assessment of a child's capabilities and progress. It would be understandable if they based their assessments mainly on 'finished' or 'public' pieces of writing – for example, the story, poem, book review, playscript or newspaper article which has gone through several drafts before reaching its final form. There may be a variety of reasons why teachers tend to assess mainly finished writing, including the quite proper wish to make assessments based on the evidence of children's best achievements. It may, indeed, seem an easier task than trying to evaluate, for example, notes or jottings. They may have little experience of using these kinds of writing as a basis for assessment and so feel that they lack a worked-out view of the criteria which might be used or the features which would indicate competence. They may be reluctant to use children's more personal, reflective writing – as seen in journals, for instance – as a basis for making comments about a child's progress in writing. No one would want to quarrel with these reservations about making evaluative judgements of certain kinds of writing. However, it is worth considering which forms of writing, and so which kinds of evidence of achievement, would not be represented if only final drafts are used for assessment.

The fact that these forms of writing are 'public' immediately suggests that the writer began with the intention of communicating her ideas to readers other than herself. Identifying and evaluating the success with which a child has fulfilled these communicative purposes is, indeed, an important area and should form a significant part of any full assessment of a young writer's capabilities. But basing assessment on finished pieces alone runs the risk of missing some important strands of any child's writing competence: those which reveal the ability to use writing as preparation for other tasks – for example, giving a talk, or making notes from information sources. 'Disposable' writing like this can offer significant evidence of how a child uses writing to structure learning, to work out ideas and to shape thought. Similarly, if those personal, reflective and evaluative forms often seen in journal writing are not included, then assessments will miss an important area of writing competence – evidence of the child's increasing control over the choices and decisions about how to use writing effectively in any particular set of circumstances. It is in these more personal kinds of writing that we often find children giving their reasons for choosing to express themselves in particular ways.

In *Writing and Learning* it is suggested that:

> Reflective writing can be a way of creating more common understanding of what learning is about. It can be used as a means of genuinely informing teachers about children's learning as well as helping pupils to reflect on what they have learned, establishing some kind of dialogue.[5]

Its seems crucial that in keeping records of progress and in making judgements about a child's capabilities in a range of forms or genres, teachers will need to make assessments of all kinds of writing – notes, jottings, drafts, journal entries, as well as finished or public writing – and to discuss these with the writers, if assessment is genuinely to lead to future progress.

A wider range of writing analysed

The samples of writing provided by Oliver, Katherine and Zoe represent some public and personal uses of writing. In looking closely at these we hope to suggest aspects of the writing which a teacher might fruitfully consider when making some assessment of a young writer's competence over a wider range of writing than looking only at final drafts would allow. Besides this, the samples are drawn from a variety of curriculum areas, not just those which might be designated 'English' or 'language' work. This, too, has implications for selection of pieces for continuing records of progress, to which we return in Chapter 4.

During the term this writing was done, Oliver was 10 and Katherine and Zoe 11. All the work arose from the theme 'Communications'. During the course of the term the class learned about electricity in Science; reading and making the news in Drama; the transmission of values through religion (in this case Hinduism) in RE. In Craft and Design they built model communicators and looked at the design of buildings. Using the *Middle English* programme *True Romance* and analysing commercials and soap opera, they examined how television portrays life and influences attitudes.

From the pieces provided by the children we selected six as representing a range of types of writing. Another factor which we took into account was writing which may pose some problems in terms of making adequate assessments of children's capabilities. The first two examples, drawn from Oliver's Science work, serve as examples of these difficulties. The first is a letter which he wrote on behalf of himself and a group of friends after they had visited a power station. In normal circumstances this letter would have left the classroom and not remained for assessment, although its draft form may have been accessible. (We have used the draft here.) The second is a poem. Many teachers express reluctance to make evaluative judgements of children's poetry. They may have inhibitions about awarding a grade or mark to something which is necessarily an expression of a child's emotional experience; or feel that because poetry is by its very nature a result of particular choices in content and language that they lack an evaluative framework to do it justice. Poems seem to come in all shapes and sizes and don't necessarily conform to any easily codified 'rules'. Both pieces, however, show what a young writer can do when using certain formal conventions. A letter is, of course, a familiar and clearly prescribed form, but because of that can be difficult to write; a poem, although perhaps giving more leeway in terms of layout, uses patterns of time and content organization which are different from narrative accounts and require some skill in working with less clearly defined conventions.

Oliver's letter (Figure 3) indicates a clear sense of the need to remind the reader of the context for the letter. It shows that he has a firm grasp of the courtesies usual for this kind of conventional communication. His poem (Figure 4) reflects an ability to create form for himself. The teacher offered the poem 'November' as a possible model for writing and Oliver successfully adapts it to his own purposes. He effectively manages to express the value of this source of power to everyday life.[6]

From both pieces it is clear that Oliver can handle different forms. He is capable of varying both the vocabulary chosen and items of content relevant to his intentions in writing and to the reader's interests. He shows that he can write personally and on behalf of others and can 'stand in other people's shoes'. He shapes and organizes his material through a confident use of time/tense indicators: in the letter he moves from past to continuous present to future; in his poem he carefully avoids any markers of time, using verbs as nouns. Most particularly, he shows a clear sense that his writing will be read by others; he has firmly grasped the fundamental point that he is a writer. In the note he enclosed with his letter to us he comments on his writing in an engaging way.

> I liked my writing when I was first writing it I was surprised when katherine & Zoe chose my poem 'No power.' I never really like writing poems but when I wrote this one I enjoyed it. My favourite line is "No video, T.V. No neighbours for me". If I ever write a poem it usally comes out totally boring, but this one was diffrent.

His honesty is disarming – 'I was surprised'; 'it usually comes out totally boring'.

These comments give us some clues about the importance of young writers being able to develop a way of evaluating and talking about their writing, factors which are dealt with in some depth in Chapter 3. Looking at the analysis from the point of view of its ability to reveal important features of non-narrative writing,

STARTING POINTS 39

Choices/intentions
- achieves intention to express gratitude in a simple, straightforward way
- selects reasons for their thanks – mentions pleasure and learning
- sustains tone of writing on behalf of others

Awareness of reader
- creates the context: starts by mentioning the tour
- recognizes that the reader has other calls on her time
- offers a courtesy/bridge to continuing contact: 'I hope we can visit again'

> Dear Madam,
> Thank you for the tour you gave us around Fawley Power ~~Stati~~ Station. We enjoyed it very much. Now we understand a bit more about electricity and how it works. Thank you for ~~~~ giving up your time. We hope we can ~~to~~ visit again
>
> Yours ~~Sincerely~~ Sincerely,
>
> Oliver, Paul, Ethan, Carl and Mark.

Form/organization
- clearly understands the letter conventions: opens with a reminder, comments about the effects of the visit, casts forward to possible future visits, closes with conventional courtesies
- uses complex time/tense organisation to shape his meaning 'we enjoyed', 'we understand', 'we hope we can . . .'

Technical features
- although in draft, surface features are almost entirely correct
- self-corrects as he drafts: revises capital letters and punctuation although there are still one or two details to deal with
- uses an effective mixture of formal, colloquial and idiomatic expression, 'now we understand', 'a bit more', 'giving up your time'
- uses simple but varied sentences

Figure 3

Choices/intentions
- fulfils intention of giving a personal response to the suggested situation: 'what would it be like if there were no electricity?'
- chooses from shared, personal experience to make his meaning clear
- catalogues the ordinary pleasures which would be missed if there were no electricity

Awareness of reader
- speaks to readers of his own age: 'you' could be a direct approach to the reader or a colloquial form
- selects items which have relevance for others, not just his own needs: refers to the swimming pool and *Neighbours*
- places himself as observer then moves to a more personal note in second section

> No power
> No light
> A dright
> No school
> No swimming pool
> No Heating
> No eating of your favorite medl
> No video, T.V.
> No Neibours for me
> No electric blanket for keeping me warm
> No power

Form/organization
- writes in clearly demarcated lines
- keeps meaning generalized by avoiding time/tense markers
- understands the visual impact of a poem's form: balances terse, short lines against more extended comments
- keeps the momentum going by internal and end of line rhyme as well as syllabic rhythm, both broken for effect in the second section

Technical features
- decides (?) not to use end-of-line punctuation, in contrast to earlier, competent sentence marking
- knows how to use full stops for abbreviation: 'T.V.'
- places comma for effective emphasis: 'no video, T.V.'
- uses repetition for effect
- chooses simple, everyday vocabulary suitable to the subject matter
- only two spelling errors

Figure 4

the framework seems to be effective. It reveals a writer who knows how to be economical: how to gain and hold the attention of different readers and control his writing through the use of complex elements of technique. Although the letter was in draft form it seems to need little further editing so that both pieces of Oliver's work can certainly be seen as 'public' and probably as 'finished'. After considering these reasonably polished, and certainly public, pieces, however, we needed to see if the framework could equally highlight features of children's competence when used to look at writing which is not intended as an end-product but as a preparation for another task.

'Disposable' writing – or is it?

Katherine's work gives us a chance to look at some of the 'disposable' writing mentioned earlier. She had carefully prepared notes for her part in a presentation to the class about the model communicator she and two friends had made. But notes like this are easily lost and may well not figure in an assessment of the range of writing a child can use. In these notes Katherine shows the ability to sustain in her mind a multiple audience – herself, her two friends who will need to read the notes, and the class she will be addressing:

Communicator

Our communicator communicates using semefore

Because we couldn't think of how to make the communicator work using electricity we made the model into lego to get a better idea of what to do.

When we had done that Mrs Phillips showed us how to make cogs out of matchsticks and wheels. After we knew how to make cogs we started to design.

It took us two attempts at designing but in the end we came up with this (hold up design)

Next we split up. Susan and Nicola made one model and Katherine made another.

How we made them

First we made two 15 by 12 cm rectangles then we made four 10 cm pieces of wood and glued them to one of the rectangular bases. After that we made two 21 cm lenths of dowel and 4 10 cm pieces of wire.

When we tried our first design we found we didn't have enough room for the cogs so we designed them again until we came up with the model we've got now.

We made the wire into 4 axle holders and fixed them onto two ten centimetre pieces of wood poking out of the rectangular base. We put the axle holders at the same level so that a piece of dowel could go through the middle.

The electricks

First of all we 'ordered'

> 30 cm of flex at 10p for 10 cm
> 2 motors at 35p
> 2 elastic bands at 2p
> 2 battries 30p a day
> 1 piece of card at 50p a piece
> and 50 5 cm pieces of masking tape at 2p a piece.

When we ordered we found that their weren't any switches left so we made one of our own out of two drawing pins and a piece of metal.

Firstly we fixed two pieces of flex into the motor. Then we fixed one of the other ends of the flex to one of the drawing pins on the switch. We then took the other end of the other piece of flex and connected it to one end of the batteries. Next we took another piece of flex and connected one end to the batteries and the other end to the switch.

Katherine shows her *intentions* and the *choices* she makes in putting the piece together as she:

- Chooses to write full notes (for partners to share? to give herself confidence?). Her list shows that she could have made her notes more succinct if she had wished.
- Gives prompts to herself (and partners?) – 'hold up design' – suggesting that she is familiar with presenting ideas for talks and knows how to select what to show.
- Sustains the dual intention to write notes helpful to herself and her partners as well as a clear enough explanation for the class audience.

She demonstrates *awareness of the reader* as she:

- Recognizes her partners' needs through prompts, and references to herself in the third person.
- Acknowledges the needs of the class audience by including full and explicit details.
- Invites the audience to share in the whole process, both the difficulties and the successes: 'it took us two attempts'; 'we came up with this'; 'when we tried our first design we found . . .'.
- Adopts the tone of confident 'expert' on her subject but makes it clear that the class members are equal in understanding by using, but not explaining, technical terms.

In terms of *form and organization* she:

- Uses subheadings – 'How we made them'; 'the electricks' and section/paragraph breaks to help make her notes clear.
- Uses time markers to show sequence of the design process: 'First . . . next . . . after that . . . when . . .'.

And she shows a good level of competence in her *technical features* as she:
- Blends colloquial and technical terms, responding to the need to communicate effectively to a familiar audience: 'to get a better idea'; 'rectangular base'; 'came up with'; 'axle holders'; 'dowel'; 'flex'.
- Varies sentence length and complexity: 'when . . . so . . .' balanced against 'Next we split up . . .'.
- Uses the apostrophe to mark omission/contraction.
- Uses inverted commas to mark usage of 'ordered' as a mathematical term.
- Makes few spelling errors in about 250 words.

All in all this is a most competent written explanation, particularly impressive in her capability to sustain awareness of a multiple audience for the writing. Again, however, our lack of context means that we cannot judge how useful the notes were for Katherine herself. In this case the notes were intended to be read by her partners, which accounts for the fullness of detail and shows her sensitive awareness of the needs of two known readers. Did she whittle the notes down for her own part of the talk? Did she need to read them verbatim rather than simply use them as a basis for talking? These questions suggest another reason for including disposable or supporting writing as well as finished pieces for assessment. Making notes is a valuable technique. For an effective classroom talk, notes need to provide relatively simple prompts so that they will not get between speaker and listener. As a means of gathering information they need not be written in full sentences; indeed, laborious copying out of source material can mean that learners have not completely understood the information they have collected. Obviously Katherine can make notes adequate for her purposes here; can she make more economical notes for other purposes? If making and using succinct and effective notes is a valuable part of a young writer's repertoire, then the techniques need to be taught and assessed as part of the child's developing competence.

Writers write about writing . . .

The second example of Katherine's writing is again in a form which might not be included in a record of progress. We had asked each of the three children who allowed us to use their work to write a brief comment on their writing. This request was made during a hurried conversation in the corridor and they were given no clearer explanation than that! We decided to look closely at Katherine's to see what a careful analysis might reveal about another form of writing which may not be seen as valid for assessment purposes. In fact, since this left the classroom immediately it was written and had not been drafted, it would have been impossible for the teacher to include it! However, reflective and self-evaluative writing does highlight important aspects of competence; perhaps teachers need to find ways of encouraging such writing and including the abilities it reveals in a full assessment of the range of a young writer's competence.[7] How might it be possible to capture comments like these?

About my writing

I find writing enjoyable especially when I write something I'm proud of. When I'm told to write a story about anything I want I find that I write something totaly unrealistic with things happeoning in them like I walked across the ceiling and met a mouse. These type of comical stories I like writing the most. If I'm given a subject to write about, my stories are usually serious and long as if I haven't finished them and that they could go on forever this is probaly because so much has happened and theres still so much to happen.

Katherine shows that she can make informed *choices* to fulfil her *intentions* as a writer as she:

- Copes well with the vague request to comment on her own writing.
- Focuses on story rather than on other forms of writing.
- Selects illustrative examples to clarify her statements: 'like I walked across the ceiling'.
- Chooses to write about what she enjoys.
- Makes a distinction between how she writes when she has a choice of subject and when a subject is given to her.

In taking account of the fact that she is writing for fairly unfamiliar *readers* she:

- Begins with a clear statement of her feelings to key the reader in to the main point (about choice) she is making.
- Gives details to help the reader understand her statements about what her stories are like: 'totaly unrealistic'; 'usually serious and long'.
- Uses deictic markers to lead the reader through her explanation: '*These* type of comical stories'; '*this* is probaly because'.

Although this is a comparatively brief piece she shows capability in *form and organization* as she:

- Divides her comments into two clear categories: chosen/given subjects.
- Begins with a confident general statement which she follows with specific reference.
- Provides examples to illustrate her point.
- Summarizes and generalizes with 'these type of comical stories'.
- Refers back by drawing contrast with the earlier example 'If I'm given'.

In terms of *technical features*, she:

- Can mark sentences appropriately but fails to do so in the final part of this example.
- Uses phrases suitable to a reflective tone: 'I find . . .'; 'this is probaly because . . .'.
- Has developed a vocabulary to comment on narrative writing: 'a story'; 'unrealistic'; 'a subject'; 'type of . . . stories'.

Although there is an interesting lapse of surface feature correctness in the final section, this piece does, indeed, reveal important features of Katherine's competence both as a writer and, importantly, as a thinker and language user more generally. It also raises some of the same questions which Oliver's self-evaluative comments raised – those related to the ways in which young writers can best be helped to develop a vocabulary through which they can effectively comment on their own writing. One significant point which is made explicit through the analysis of Katherine's writing, though only reflected obliquely in the other children's writing, is her awareness of story genre. By our request for her to comment on her writing she is able to demonstrate her awareness of certain typical and general features of story, using the language of narrative analysis – 'subject'; 'unrealistic'; 'these type of comical stories'. She also implies that she understands the need for a clear narrative thread where in her final section she tries to unpick what she sees as faults in her own construction of narrative. Is it too fanciful to assume that her control over conventions of syntax and punctuation fall apart a little here because she is, in fact, thinking as she writes, trying to work out what she wants to explain about her writing?

There is another aspect of writing revealed in this short piece, too – something about what being a writer in a classroom is like. Her deliberate distinction between chosen and given subjects indicates that she knows that writing can spring from different sources and that the origins of a story can influence both subject matter and structure. Katherine is knowledgeable about her own abilities and is well on the way to making improvements to her story writing with sensitive intervention from the teacher. Both pieces show that she can stand back from her writing and use it as a means of organizing ideas – for herself and others. Her letter gives us valuable information about her own understanding of what it is to be a writer and raises the question of how teachers might offer pupils similar opportunities.

. . . and about being readers

In Zoe's letter she, too, tells us a great deal about what happens when she writes. Despite her reservations about English as a separate part of the curriculum, she is able to comment perceptively about her writing. She begins:

> Dear Mrs Bern,
> I don't like English much but once I get going ideas seem to pour out of my mind one after the other. I am pleased with my myth and diaster work. I did not feel pleased with 'true romance' work which I did.

It is interesting that both she and Katherine acknowledge the difficulties of capturing a flow of thoughts in writing. Having a chance to work through several drafts is one way of making sure that writing will express just about everything you want it to, and Zoe's work gives us a chance to see what happens when a writer has the opportunity to redraft. She sent us both her draft for the newspaper story based on the 'disaster' work she did in Drama and the final word-processed text, see opposite page. A comparison between the two raises some interesting points.

In terms of the analytical framework she makes some important choices. As a focus for the theme of 'disaster' she chooses to take the plight of one survivor and make it a personal news story. She makes strenuous attempts to maintain the genre of journalistic writing by choosing language to suggest drama and urgency: 'the cyclone--hit village'; 'her ordeal'. This evocative language is suitable to newspaper reporting – 'shacks'; 'debris'; 'ripped' – and she heightens the sense of disaster by deciding to place the fall as the cyclone was approaching so that 'her cries were drowned by the wind'.

Zoe acknowledges the distant readership suitable for a newspaper report as she raises and sustains the interest by dramatic detail. She sets the scene in the first sentence to key the reader in then keeps the pace going throughout, ending with the 'human interest' detail of her injuries and fears for her family. This approach is particularly appropriate to the genre. She take the tone of an excited but objective reporter and does not explicitly include the readership any further than by enticing them to read on by her use of dramatic detail.

She organizes the piece fairly well in its draft form but marks it for some reorganization. She handles the time/tense variation to great effect, setting a chronological past tense account within the continuous present appropriate to news reporting. Her alterations show that she can reread and edit her own work, adding details which she detects that the reader will need in order to understand the sequence of events and which she missed as she worked quickly to get her original ideas down.

Even in draft form her technical competence is clear. She marks sentences accurately even though she is rushing to capture her first thoughts and can deal consistently with reported speech. She handles complex sentence structure competently in dealing with reporting conventions; this is noticeable in the verb forms she uses and her use of subordinate clauses. Her revisions show that she can recognize her own error and successfully reach conventional spelling.

Zoe changed her original draft when she typed it on to the word processor. At first sight there do not seem to be many amendments, but closer analysis shows the extent of the changes she made. They seem to fall into three categories: changes made for consistency; changes made for clarity; and changes made for dramatic effect. All of these show her capacity to take into account the needs of a reader.

Zoe has noticed that her phrase 'concerned about her family and friends' is not

~~Mis~~ a survivior
Miss Zoé Craig ~~of~~ who lives in the
"~~cyclone hit village Batp told me what her~~"
Cyclone hit village Batpura told what
her ~~ad~~ ordeal was like.
   She was working in the fields
when she saw the III ran to the hotel for
   shelter but she tripped over and
some debri fell ~~over~~ on her. it was getting wet and windy. shacks and trees
were falling down around her. her cries
for help wer drowned by the wind.
She saw her home and possessions
were washed away by the flood.
"cyclone coming and" she suffered from
   a broken leg, 3 bruised ribs and a ~~distoct~~
~~dis~~ dislocated shoulder, she is worried
  about her family and friends and is

TODAY
31 1 89 18P

CYCLONE HITS INDIAN VILLAGE

Miss Zoe Craig a survivior who lives in the cyclone--hit Indian village Batpura told us what her ordeal was like. She was working in the fields when she saw the cyclone coming. She was running to the hotel for shelter when she tripped and fell. Shacks and trees were falling down around her. Some debris fell on her and her cries for help were drowned by the wind. It was getting wet and the cyclone was getting worse. The tin roof of the hotel was ripped off. It was nearly four hours before she was rescued and rushed to hospital. She suffered from a broken leg, three bruised ribs and a dislocated shoulder. She is now recovering in hospital and is very concerned about her future.

HUNDREDS KILLED

WIN A FREE SAFARI IN DISENY WORLD!

connected with any earlier mention of family so, for the sake of consistency, she changes it to 'concerned for her future'. Similarly she omits 'she saw her home and possessions washed away by the flood'.

She adds detail to give the reader important contextual information, for example inserting 'Indian' in the first sentence. However, one editorial decision she makes for clarity involves quite considerable reorganization of information. From the original:

> but she tripped and some debri fell on her. it was getting wet and windy. shacks and trees were falling down around her. her cries for help were drowned by the wind.

she reorganizes the text to read:

> She tripped and fell. Shacks and trees were falling down around her. Some debris fell on her and her cries for help were drowned by the wind. It was getting wet and the cyclone was getting worse.

She achieves dramatic effect by changing 'windy' into 'the cyclone was getting worse'. In addition, she adds phrases like 'it was nearly four hours', 'rushed to hospital', and 'the tin roof of the hotel was ripped off', all of which add to the drama and urgency of the piece.

These represent just a few of the revisions she has made, but looking closely at them raises another issue about assessment. We have suggested that it is important to include 'disposable' writing in any full assessment of a writer's repertoire. Zoe's draft and word-processed article add another dimension. If we are to make full and balanced evaluations about what children can do with writing we need the evidence provided by a comparison like this. What do Zoe's editorial changes tell us about her understanding of what is needed to make her meaning clear? About the competence she is demonstrating in making choices as she adds to or deletes from her original piece? About her capacity to be an attentive and critical reader of her own writing? All of these features would be lost if only her word-processed text were used for assessment.

Issues of content . . . and discontent

In her letter Zoe said that she was not pleased with her 'True Romance' work although she gave no details. As the final example which we analyse in this chapter, this work gives us a chance to look at another question about selecting pieces of writing for continuing assessment. The class had been watching the television *Middle English* series about romantic fiction and they had been asked to rewrite the ending of the story they had watched. The first piece of Zoe's writing is a set of notes, responded to by her teacher:

True Romance

① Paula could have come on to stage.
② he could have made ~~fr~~ friends with Andrex
③ Andrex could have followed him to Liverpool if car hadn't come.
④ When he opened the door his mum could have been standing at the door
③ ~~Afte~~ he could have found
⑤ mum and Andrex could of run up to him and kissed him

The teacher responds:

You have suggested a number of possible endings here. Choose one and write the new end for the story based on that one idea.

The second piece shows her attempt to write more fully:

> **True Romance**
> When Beetle said he was going back to Liverpool, Andrex decided to follow him so she quickly ran home and ~~sa~~ packed some things and got some money. She ~~r~~ ran outside and saw Beetle getting on a Bus. She got on the Bus, and sat behind Beetle. the Bus stopped in Liverpool. Beetle got off. Andrex followed him. Beetle saw his mum, and ran over to ~~him~~ her. Andrex ran up to him and kissed him.

The teacher asks:

> How did Beetle feel about finding mum? Was he pleased Andrex had followed him?

and she replies:

> Beetle pleased that he found Mum and he felt happy and wanted again
>
> Beetle did like Andrex following him at first but when Andrex said she fancied him he was even more happy.

We have throughout tried to use our framework to identify only positive features of children's writing. Zoe was not pleased with this piece, and it certainly does not reveal her capabilities as a writer as much as her 'disaster' piece – nor as much as in her letter to us. She seems to be merely fulfilling a task rather than becoming involved with what she is writing about. This is particularly suggested by the amount of prompting her teacher has to do. First, however, we looked at what she showed that she could do in this piece.

She understands and uses the convention of the genre of 'happy ending' romance stories. At the same time, she is capable of combining several ideas from her original while maintaining a story thread involving three characters showing some sophistication in her intentions in writing this piece. Although her main difficulties seem to lie in the area of what readership to write for, she does give important details in the first sentence which help a reader understand what the story is about. Also she responds to questions posed by the teacher. The form follows a visually descriptive chronological account and she is able to add details of characterization when prompted by the teacher. Even in draft form her technical competence is shown by the marking of sentences accurately and the use of commas for clause boundary pauses. This draft shows evidence of reading back and revising: 'and saw' becomes 'packed'; 'him' becomes 'her'; she inserts 'was' in the final line.

However, there are several problems posed here. The first is to do with selection of pieces for assessment. Zoe was not happy with the writing. When making an overall evaluation of a young writer's competence, where should a piece feature which is considered by the writer to be unsuccessful? We have no hard and fast answer to that except to suggest that even unsatisfactory writing can reveal positive indications of competence as shown in the analysis. Decisions about selection of particular pieces can only be adequately made by the teacher who has access to the full range of the child's writing, often in consultation with the child herself. If, as this piece suggests, and as Katherine hinted in her letter, a developing writer sometimes finds a set task in writing difficult to handle, what are the implications for the classroom?[8]

Closer to home, perhaps, there is a second problem raised by Zoe's 'True Romance' writing – one of content and genre. Zoe has obliged the teacher by providing an ending to the love story; she has obeyed the convention which she has probably drawn from her reading and television viewing that stories like these should end happily. More than this, she has followed the storyline and characters created by the television series and the result is perhaps more suggestive of stereotype than of fully fleshed-out characters behaving realistically. Her organization of the material into a visually descriptive account in chronological order seems to indicate her following the television form. This brings into focus another aspect related to evaluation of a young writer's work. When faced with a piece like this, considered unsatisfactory by the writer, appearing to the reader to be rather flat and lifeless, and possibly suggesting gender stereotypes which could be challenged, what does the teacher do? Part of the value of assessment lies in the information it gives the teacher for forward planning. Seeing what a young writer can already do provides a basis for looking at how she can be helped to develop ideas and techniques in writing. In Chapter 4 we look at some issues of content, but certainly it seems that Zoe's work would benefit from discussions with her teacher about the picture she presents here.

Gemma Moss, in her book *Un/Popular Fictions*, suggests some specific ways that teachers can use content which they may regard as questionable to help developing writers move forward. More than this, she suggests that the adult's view may stand in the way of recognizing how a girl may be working out her own views of gender roles through writing in what may seem to be narrowly stereotypical forms. She points out that 'Writing alone does not shape what we think. We bring what we know to the text and try to push it into shape.' There are important implications for teachers who accept that their pupils are struggling to create meaning out of a mass of personal experiences and feelings, other texts and the present writing task:

> we should broaden our notions of what constitutes useful and interesting writing, and include within that definition writing based on popular fiction. . . . We could encourage children to articulate what they already know about how such fictions work and help to refine that knowledge.[9]

Rather than suggesting that this piece has 'let Zoe down' it is perhaps more fruitful to see it as showing the way to possible growth in Zoe's development as a writer, reader and thinker. She has shown some understanding of the genre of 'True Romance' stories; how can she be helped to develop a more confidently critical stance which will give her a chance to make her own meanings clear? This has relevance for the issues raised earlier about children's knowledge about language. Clearly Zoe has a great deal of implicit knowledge about text organization and genre. Talking and writing about texts – both those she reads and those she writes – will help her realize and make clear to herself just what she does know. This in turn will help her recognize her own views about reading and writing.

A clearer view of progress

Looking carefully at children's writing as we have in this chapter has not only shown present competence but also has been a chance to consider past experience and future possibilities. The framework has not only identified what four young writers can do as they write for different reasons, but also pinpointed some common areas worthy of inclusion in any evaluation of writing.[10] The categories which we used suggest some insights might lead to a clearer description of progress.

Choices/intentions

Each of the pieces reflects strong influences from other experiences – from earlier practice or from other texts. All of the writers, in their notes, letters or responses to their teacher's writing, indicate that: they expect others to read their writing for the meaning it conveys; they come to writing knowing that they can include their own thoughts and experiences as worthy of attention; and they make choices about what to include based on previous experience, combined with the impact they want to make and the meanings they want to convey. These insights carry important implications not only for evaluation but also for classroom practice. If young writers are to be in a position to fulfil their own intentions in writing they need both opportunities and experiences which will support and extend their efforts to make meaning for themselves. This suggests not only experience of different genres or models for writing but also that young writers should be offered the challenge of deciding what is needed in terms of content to serve their purposes for specific occasions for writing.

Awareness of the reader

As well as giving a chance to notice that each writer makes particular choices about how to write, it is clear that each piece takes into account who it is written for. In other words, it acknowledges the needs of the reader. All of the examples reveal the skill with which the writers include their readership, either by direct invitation or by giving information which will key the reader in to what the writing is about. The analysis meant that we could identify just how they went about this, and could see that all four expected their writing to be read for the meaning it carried, rather than simply being 'corrected' as a more or less accurate technical exercise. Again there are important messages about classroom writing here. If one significant feature of development is an increasing ability to vary the tone of writing according to who is likely to read it, then the more opportunities to write for different readers, including the writer herself, the better. It raises the question of how classrooms can best be organized to encourage a variety of experiences of readership.

These two categories of the analysis show that an important part of evaluation lies in looking for clues about the success with which writers signal their communicative intentions. It is equally important to be able to detect just how they do this.

Form/organization

All of the examples show varying degrees of control over text organization – for example, the way that time/tense markers show different ways of organizing material. The decisions the writers make about what they want to write and who they expect to read their writing are closely interwoven with how they set about the work in hand. Once again, earlier experience and other models can be seen reflected in each piece. In the texts we have looked at here, we can see young writers getting to grips with form and genre in ways which not only suggest past influences but also signal future possibilities. We may not know just how Oliver came to understand the conventions involved in constructing a letter of thanks, or that a poem can be written within particular conventions while still expressing personal and shared experience, though we may guess. Similarly, we cannot tell how Katherine learned about making notes or Zoe took on the genre features of news story writing. The fact that they are working within these forms, confidently trying out their own voices, is itself important. It emphasizes the need for young writers to experience a wide variety of forms of writing and reading. It points to the importance of seeing all kinds of writing – public and private, finished and disposable – as valid for inclusion in any continuing assessment. More than this, it strengthens the need to encourage young writers to look carefully at their own writing, as well as at other writers' work, to see if they have managed to achieve their intentions and just how they did it.

Technical features

It is clear that all four writers are technically competent and this has given us the chance to look closely at features of syntax, choice of vocabulary, punctuation and spelling. The evidence of self-correcting, revising and editing shows how effective young writers can be as readers and critics of their own writing. Looking at the range of punctuation each has used to shape sentences, give emphasis, create echoes of inflection, for example, suggests how reading a variety of forms of writing and paying explicit attention to how these pieces are put together can powerfully influence young writers' potential for experimenting with their own texts. In Chapter 5 we consider children's knowledge about language in more detail. Certainly, the evidence of implicit knowledge is here alive and kicking in the few examples we have looked at and suggests that helping developing writers recognize this knowledge would be an effective way of broadening technical scope.

One point which struck us most forcibly about the more formal and technical features of the writing examples is to do with power. All four writers reveal a high level of control over their material and a sense that they have the power to make meaning through the construction of their writing as well as what they choose to write about. Zoe's drafting shows this in action. Intentions for writing are interwoven with the organization of writing. Decisions made about the one are determined by the power to express ideas in a form which will best carry the meaning. This has implications for the ways in which looking at what children can do now gives us clues about how we can help them move on. All of the writers show that they are actively involved with the content and the form of their writing, consciously shaping it so that it will get their messages across. This awareness of power is a significant factor in development and challenges us to see how we can best support and extend the power of young writers as they grapple with the demands they make on themselves as active constructors of meaning.

The framework we have used is an attempt to begin to untangle some of the strands which make up a piece of writing in order to describe more accurately the wide array of competences young writers bring to their writing. Putting the strands together again can illuminate the process further.[11] Taken separately, the four categories allow observations of particular features of writing competence. Viewed together they clarify the picture. They can allow comparison across varying forms of writing by one child or between pieces of writing by different children. Significantly, however, they move our attention from the writing alone towards a wider view of the conditions needed for writers to develop further.

The circle of literacy

Through close reading of children's writing we have raised some questions about continuing evaluation. When trying to give a full picture of a writer's capabilities what forms of writing should be included? What effect does the classroom context have on writing? What about choice? And what about writing which fails to satisfy both writer and reader? When making a full assessment it is clear that we need to take into account past and future possibilities. The writers who have let us use their work as a starting point for thinking about progress in writing have learned from their teachers that their writing matters; they have come to see themselves as writers. Their texts give very clear indications of the possible ways in which their writing can develop if they are given further opportunities to experiment, to read and to comment on their own and others' writing, to discuss matters of content and use of language. In her letter, Zoe pointed out that when she gets going 'ideas seem to pour out of my mind one after the other'; how could Zoe and others like her be helped to maintain the flow of ideas but form them into writing which will be satisfying? Much of this depends on the way in which the teacher observes and responds to writing, plans and creates a classroom environment which will be supportive and challenging.

Assessment of progress is part and parcel of the teacher's continuing process of organizing for learning. The interventions she makes in terms of conversations, response to writing and setting up classroom opportunities will be linked with her evaluation of children's development. It is reassuring, though, that she will not be working alone; the capacities for self-evaluation shown by the four writers we have focused on in this chapter give a clear promise that by working together, teachers and pupils can identify, discuss and record the process of development. As we have emphasized, much of that process is bound up with the experiences of literacy which young writers call upon as they form and shape writing for their own purposes. Several of the pieces of writing we have looked at in this chapter give clues about the effect reading both verbal and visual text has on young writers who are experimenting with what they can do in writing. Zoe's letter makes it clear that reading is very important to her:

> Some ideas I got for my myth from Seasons of Splendour, a book of Indian myths. I got it from our school library. I read lots of books, and my mum says that I should write more stories being as I read so much. I go to our local library every week and I get four books, which is the maximum I can get out on my library ticket. I mostly get books out of the teenage section because I have read most of the children's books. I will be going to the Hurst community school, Baughurst Hill, Baughurst, nr Basingstoke, Hants, in September.

Children's literacy experiences feed into their writing in a powerful way. Taking the cue from Zoe, in the next chapter we step into the classroom to hear the voices of children whose reading was a starting point for writing, who are learning to become more attentive and critical readers of their own writing and who are gaining in confidence as they capture the flow of ideas and give them form in writing.

Notes

1 We have deliberately chosen to use the word 'intentions' here since it better reflects what we want to identify. 'Purposes' can be either the teacher's *or* the child's. Since we want to emphasize the writer's own decisions about writing, we focus on choice and intention. A writer's intentions can be detected through looking at amendments and additions; choices of form, sentence organization; selection of vocabulary and extent of formality used.
2 While working for the School Curriculum Development Committee's National Writing Project during the period 1985–8 we took part in many discussions, seminars and workshops where teachers and co-ordinators considered the question of how to offer an adequate description of progress in writing.

3 It is often difficult to decide what pieces of writing to select for assessment and continuing record-keeping. Chapter 4 deals with this in detail and suggests a simple format for compiling a folder of work with evaluative comments.
4 Chapter 5 includes examples of work done by Steven's class when they were aged 8 and 9. From this it is clear how Steven and his friends began to understand that their writing would be read for its meaning.
5 From Nelson/National Writing Project, 'Reflecting and Responding' in *Writing and Learning*, Kingston, Nelson (1988), p. 37.
6 If colleagues wanted to work together to discuss writing development it might be useful to take Oliver's poem, or any of the pieces in this chapter, remove the analytical comments and see what the group can come up with themselves within the categories. Other useful ideas for colleagues working together on the development of writing policy can be found in Nelson/National Writing Project, *Making Changes*, Kingston, Nelson (1990), which is a collection of activities designed to help teachers examine a range of issues about writing and classrooms.
7 Later chapters emphasize the importance of encouraging young writers to become reflective about their own writing. Encouraging children to write about writing is one of the most effective ways to help them articulate their ideas, questions and ambitions about their own attempts. In terms of what this reveals about children's knowledge about language such writing is invaluable to the teacher who is seeking to provide an environment of challenge and support to developing writers.
8 Chapter 3 provides a much fuller examination of the effect of choice on children's success in writing.
9 G. Moss, *Un/Popular Fictions*, London, Virago Education Series (1987), p. 117.
10 For an alternative approach to studying progress in writing, see R. Arnold, *Writing Development: magic in the brain*, Milton Keynes, Open University Press (1991), where the author takes rather different categories to make a longitudinal study of just a few young writers, suggesting an alternative approach to assessment from the one we provide here.
11 Looking at the two categories we have placed side by side at the top of the framework, *choices/intentions* and *awareness of reader*, gives a strong picture of a writer's communicative effectiveness. Seeing *form/organization* and *technical features* together shows just how skilful writers can be in fulfilling the demands of their own intentions. Similarly, looking at the two left-hand categories together indicates how intentions in writing are closely bound up with the experience of possible forms which are available to a writer and which spring from earlier experience of reading and writing. Combining the two right-hand categories indicates how a writer uses techniques of syntax, use of vocabulary, punctuation and spelling for clarity, emphasis or presenting information in sequence; all of these strategies help the reader understand the meanings conveyed in the text.

3 The writing environment

In the previous chapter, we looked at some examples of the range of writing produced by the 10- and 11-year-olds in Sue Phillips's class. Now we are going to look at a class of 8- and 9-year-olds, focusing in particular on the classroom situation: the writing environment fostered by the teacher and the ways in which this environment enabled the children to develop a growing awareness of themselves as writers. Cath describes the classroom and the children's experiences.

Setting the scene

The scene is a class of thirty-four 8- and 9-year-olds towards the end of the summer term. Children are engaged in a variety of activities, writing, painting, doing maths and science. Andrew and David are sitting at a tape recorder. At a signal from them, the teacher warns the rest of the class to keep the noise level low as the two boys are about to tape. Children move around on tiptoe, chairs are moved carefully so that they do not scrape, sneezes are stifled.

With Andrew's help David reads his story, 'The Man and the Giant', aloud. They have the following conversation.

Andrew: What would you like to do better about the story?
David: I would like to write it out a bit better and do some more bits to it
Andrew: Are you going to try to do it on the computer or on paper?
David: I would like to do it on the computer.
Andrew: I think you have used your imagination a lot because people usually think giants are mean, don't they? and the giant helped a man and everything. It's a bit strange, isn't it?
David: Yes.
Andrew: I'll tell you one problem about it. I think you should take out some of the 'and's. Right?
David: Yes.

David moves off to put his name on the list for using the computer.

The children in this class are used to showing their writing to whomever they choose, and David no doubt asked Andrew to respond to the first draft of his story, knowing that Andrew is a more confident writer than he is and that he is a sensitive friend whom he can trust not to mock his attempts. In fact, Andrew responds in a rather didactic way to the proliferation of 'and's, but he does see in the content of David's story an element of worth remarking upon, which I might well have missed – the reversal of the usual image of a giant being a 'baddy'. This response raises David's self-esteem and confidence as a writer and demonstrates the responder's own awareness of story genre.

Later that day Alex and Stuart use the tape recorder to discuss Stuart's story, 'The Time Travellers'. They discuss the idea of putting it into a book. Since it is very short, Alex suggests that Stuart uses a previous story, to make a two-story book. The conversation continues in this way:

Stuart: To make it better. What do you think I could do, Alex? . . . to start making it better?
Alex: Um . . . here . . .
Stuart: . . . make more sense? 'Stuart and Andrew jumped on their motor bike and went . . .'.
Alex: No but here, where she finds the others. You don't say that the other person's changed.
Stuart: Yeah.
Alex: She's changed speaking to another person.
Stuart: True. True. I shall make that sound different. Any other changes that could be made?
Alex: Umm . . . Right at the end because I should have thought they'd have a bit more adventures in it.
Stuart: No. I just made them go back. I might just write a very short . . .
Alex: Ah, but with the first one it will be quite long, won't it? With 'Alien Attack'.
Stuart: 'Alien Attack' then straight on the 'The Time Travellers' and then if I just finish the story I'm writing right now, which I haven't named, I could make a three-story book.

The problem which Alex identified in Stuart's story was that a new person had started talking without the author using punctuation to make it clear that this was so – a common problem in children's written narrative, and one which Stuart would have been unlikely to spot on his own.

These two boys are evenly matched as far as writing development is concerned and regard each other as valuable partners, sometimes writing in collaboration with each other. Their talk reveals a sense of familiarity with each other and with the task. This is an everyday task which they are used to performing.

Anna and Caroline move to the tape recorder next. They have written a contribution to the class guide to the local parish church. Their piece is about the Lady Chapel. Caroline reads it then goes on to say:

> We thought we had put a lot of expression and we thought that the piece of writing was particularly good because it's a bit sad . . . all this . . . men fought in the war. I like the bit where it says they all fought for the freedom of us . . . We did this together. We thought it was a really good piece of work.

The girls also have a sense of the achievement which comes through collaboration. Their writing had a clear purpose and their satisfaction results from the content of their writing as much as from the writing itself.

The children in this class are coming to the end of their time with me as their teacher. The tape recorder is available to them to report on books they have read and enjoyed, to record the interchange between two response partners and to record their evaluations of a recent piece of writing of their own. This last task was one I expected them to do once a fortnight, although some did it voluntarily more often. All three of these tasks could also be performed in writing.

At about this time in the school year, written comments about their own pieces of work included:

> It sounded like you were there   (Anna)

> I was pleased with the end   (John)

> I was not pleased with it because the way it sounds is wierd   (Caroline)

These children are by now confident writers. They are used to writing collaboratively or alone and to having varying degrees of autonomy about what they write with rules and guidelines being laid down more firmly at some times than at others. They have a strong sense of audience and are used to their work being read by their peers, others in the school and people outside school as well as their teacher. They are beginning to develop a vocabulary with which to discuss their own and other people's writing. Words like beginning, end, drafting, description, explaining, expression, detail, theme, are becoming part of their everyday vocabulary.

This state of affairs was not reached overnight, however. I had been working towards it right from the beginning of the school year. To tell the story of how they reached this point in developing their self-criticism, I need to go back to the previous September. I will do this and try to outline the strategies which have helped them become autonomous, self-critical writers.

In *English for Ages 5 to 16* we are told: 'Teachers will have diverse roles to play in the development of young writers: they will be observers, facilitators, modellers, readers and supporters.'[1]

Teachers as facilitators

As facilitators, teachers need to provide:

- models;
- an atmosphere where risks can be taken without fear of reproach or recrimination;

- audiences which treat their writing seriously;
- the feeling that they are apprentices working alongside other apprentices;
- the chance for children to discuss their writing during the composing stage with other interested people, adults or peers;
- the insight to appraise their own and each others' writing;
- the vocabulary with which to do this.

In order that their writing should develop, children need to read. As they write, their competence in reading develops since they read their own writing critically. Reading and writing are inextricably linked, with competence in the one furthering competence in the other.

The Programme of Study for Reading Key Stage 1 states that reading materials should include, as well as the wide range of fiction and non-fiction texts, 'material which relates to the real world, such as labels, captions, notices, children's newspapers, books of instructions, plans and maps, diagrams, computer print-out and visual display'.[2] I believe that in addition to making this wide variety of texts available to children, we should clearly demonstrate to them that it is a perfectly legitimate activity for them to read any of them; that reading non-fiction is as admissible as reading fiction, comics as stories, poems as longer texts. To reinforce this attitude, and to ensure that all children experience a wide variety of genres, the teacher needs to read aloud from as many of them as possible.

This leads to the question of who chooses the text to be read aloud and of what follows such reading? Many of the texts read to a class by a teacher are chosen by that same teacher, and understandably so, in order to ensure that children hear a wide variety of texts. However, children often feel a greater sense of interest in a text which has been chosen by themselves or one of their peers.

At the beginning of that school year, I invited the children to choose poems suitable for reading aloud to the class. If, in their reading, they came across a poem which they enjoyed and thought the rest of the class would enjoy, they were to put a slip of paper in the book marking the place and leave it on a designated spot on my desk. I would make a time each day when I would pick up one of the books on the pile, having had a quick look at it first, and read the chosen poem. I would invite the child who had chosen it to comment on their choice if they wished, read the poem aloud myself, then invite comments from the class. In the discussion that followed, the children would explore ways of describing the effectiveness of the poems they heard. Gradually, with my help, they began to develop the appropriate vocabulary. I would take any opportunities presented to me to make relevant teaching points about aspects of poetry such as rhyme, rhythm, alliteration, imagery. The children's understanding of poetry began to develop, they were able to compare the poem of the day with ones they had previously met and sometimes further work, initiated by me or by the children themselves, would be done on a poem – 'We could write one like it' or 'That would make a good painting' were suggestions made by the children at different times. This was not the only way I used of presenting poetry to the children, but I was pleased with its success and grateful for the opportunity to broaden my knowledge of the sort of poem which children of that age enjoy.

With prose, I also made sure that whenever I read aloud to them, they had a chance to respond. At the beginning of the year it would need a few leading questions by me – 'Why do you think she did that?', 'What do you think will happen next?' – in order to elicit a response from the children, but these soon became unnecessary.

Another strategy I used, which served two purposes, was to use the children as experts in evaluating fiction books. I belong to a fiction study group run by the local schools librarian, where teachers have the opportunity to take new books into their classrooms to try out with the children. As I ran the school library, it was indeed very useful to know which books appealed to the children in my class. They were only too pleased to give me their opinions, either briefly in writing or verbally. The fact that their opinions were of use to me became clear when they saw me put copies of the books they had recommended into the school library.

All this work I felt to be essential in its own right in developing the children's critical faculties with regard to published texts. I also used it, however, to help the children develop ways of evaluating their own and their peers' writing.

Teachers as readers

The experiences of teachers involved in the National Writing Project showed that as much as possible of the writing that children do in class should be seen by them to be purposeful. If this is to be so, then the teacher must behave as a real reader of their writing, resisting the temptation to comment only on the presentation or technical accuracy and reading instead for meaning: commenting, praising, giving constructive criticism. Any child's text should be treated seriously, taking into account the writer's intentions, the way it is composed, the success with which meaning is communicated and the sense of audience shown by the writer. The teacher needs to make it clear that any suggestions she makes are only suggestions and that the writer has the right to accept or reject the proposed changes. This is difficult to do, since it seems natural to a child to do what the teacher says, but it is a vital part of the teacher's role if the atmosphere of apprenticeship is to be maintained.

> The people that told you about the rockests were in a pretend rocket. and at the end "they said" next week we are going to the moon.

It is vital for the writer's confidence that mistakes, failures and difficulties should be seen as temporary setbacks or even positive opportunities for learning, not as occasions for reproof or reprimand. It is useful if the teacher has the skill to recognize the reason behind a fault. It may be that the writer is trying out a new structure and that what is at first sight a mistake is, in fact, a sign of growth. In the piece reproduced on the previous page, Melanie shows that she has noticed the use of speech marks in her reading. I was able to capitalize on her interest and help her decide where her speech marks should be.

With my class, therefore, I did my best to abide by this philosophy. I provided opportunities for the children to write in as many different ways as possible. They wrote letters, poems, stories, reports, descriptions, a guide to the local church. The letters were sent to the people for whom they were intended and the poems and stories were displayed in the classroom or elsewhere in the school or 'published' and made into books which were put in the classroom or in the school library. I made a point of always discussing with the children, before they embarked upon a piece of writing, where it would finally end up. I made sure my initial response to the first draft was a positive one and that any criticism was constructive:

> He ran back down and started to make a raft when he had finished the murchets saw them shap puled the crew abord the raft and left the island. And lived at see
>
> Well done, Ian, You got a good feeling of excitement to the story. I am glad they got away!

That is not to say that I took no interest in the presentation of a final piece of writing. The understanding was that we attended to the content first and dealt with the surface features as the last step before the final draft. The children accepted that if their writing was going to be read by a wide audience, within or even outside the school, it had to be spelt and punctuated correctly and written in neat, clear handwriting or printed on the computer.

Alongside introducing the children to the idea of my assuming the role of 'helpful expert', I also introduced them to the idea of using each other as fellow apprentices. I explained to them the concept of 'response partners' and invited them to make suggestions about how to choose such a person. After some discussion, certain criteria were agreed. To qualify as a useful response partner you needed to be: someone respected by the writer; someone the writer could trust; someone whose attitude was likely to be sympathetic; and someone who wasn't at the time engaged on another absorbing task or an activity with the teacher. The children quickly got used to the system, showing common sense about who was likely to be useful to them and accepting with good grace any situation where their first choice of partner was unavailable. I found that the way in which the children collaborated in discussing each other's work provided as many learning opportunities for the 'responder' as for the writer.

To begin with, however, they needed help with the task of having to respond to the piece of writing of another child in the class. I talked to them about picking out the good parts in a piece of writing and about suggesting improvements.

I hoped that my earlier modelling of how to respond to a piece of writing would help the responders find words with which to express themselves. In order to ensure that the children showed their work to someone else before I saw it, I made it clear that I didn't want to see the draft of a piece of writing unless there was evidence of a response partner having seen it. Some response partners wrote their own comments

Lived Happy again.

I like The paRt
when The custurd
man said sorry
is it was
a BumBee RiDe.

Daniel
i Like the mowster It was very ~~fafru~~ Funny and

The Writing Environment 65

but in most cases the writer wrote down their partner's reaction for themselves.

> It's like two people dancing and prancing every-where.
>
> David Howard said I like the bit about it keeps smiling at me.

> My pattern
>
> The colours that are used in my pattern are yellow red & blue. In my pattern I can see a tiger it reminds me of a squril. The whole picture to me reminds me of a butterfly it also reminds me of my holiday in France when I looked down on the beach. There all so is a shape on here which reminds me of a chip basket. To cool down your chips. The blue bits to me remind me of counties on a map. On the side there is some splashes of blue it reminds me of light rain.
>
> Anna Rooney
> Thought the bit was good when I was looking down from the rocks in france

Martin, a confident talker but very much aware of his limitations in written language, clearly demonstrated his enthusiasm for the task of responding to Karen's writing:

> I showed my blot patter to martin.
> 'martin said" in the middle of the paper you said the patter looks like a frog I think it looks like a stick insect. In the middle of the butter-fly there looks like theres two eyes, and the dog looks like a pig. he also said I think its true about theres lots of bushes.

I found the comments so far interesting, but I somehow felt the children were inhibited in their responses to each other's writing. Maybe they didn't want to upset their peers by seeming to criticize, or maybe they simply didn't possess the means to pinpoint areas for improvement.

My next step was to ask the children to comment for themselves on their own writing when it was completed. This produced an immediate sense of engagement in some of the children which was lacking in their responses to each other's work. Although some of them, as Kristina does here, simply expressed satisfaction (and why not!)

> I like advencer storys I am qutte prode of it I liked the octopus and the nun.

others, like Jenny, showed they were far from pleased and were able to identify the weaknesses.

> I liked it where the snowman gave Richard things to eat. I liked the end. I liked the bit where Richard put a face on his snowman. I didn't like the begining so much.

This sometimes led to a dialogue with me, as this example of Melanie's shows,

> I think it good but a bit boring I think the bit where you made the house fram supper glue was silly. I think the bit about the tree wich had monkey was good. I want to put it in a book.
>
> I thought it was good. i disagree with Melanie i think the tree house sounded good. i think it should go in a book.
>
> I liked the idea of the tree house I am not sure why you built a wall round the tree. Do you really think you would have been happy there? We Built the wall so no one else could see it.
> I was happy there becouse I dident always live in the house

or even with a parent, like this from Nick:

> I Think I could of explaind what totty ~~bany~~ a trunky looked like and ~~made~~ ~~of~~ made the Aventures smaller. Nick.T.

> I think Nick could describe things in more detail and think more carefully about the adventures. Otherwise a very good effort. D.T.

> There are some very good parts to the story. I particularly like the opening with the description of the monster. I am not sure that you did need to describe the other three. It would have been nice to know how they got to the

Kristina's comment, above, shows her awareness of the genre of adventure story writing. Jenny recognizes the need for an opening which sets the scene and leads the reader into the narrative. Melanie recognizes the incongruity of introducing superglue as a way of sticking the parts of her house together, and Nick acknowledges the need to keep the audience in mind and to concentrate on fewer, rather than more, adventures in a story.

Looking back at the year's work and sorting through the children's writing to find examples, I now realize that it was at the point when I introduced the idea of the children writing their own evaluations that the atmosphere of apprenticeship, which I had aimed to foster, suddenly sprang to life. Many writers do, in fact, find it easier to revise and edit their own writing. Why should children be different?

For some considerable time the routine in the classroom had been, as far as writing was concerned, predictable. The writers knew the purpose behind and the audience for each piece of writing they began. It became a matter of course for them to write an evaluation of their own and then consult a response partner. The advice offered by the partner could be acted upon or not, as the writer saw fit. Lastly they showed the writing to me. As far as possible my responses were made verbally, although I always put my observations in writing also. Matters of presentation were dealt with before and during the final draft.

Children as evaluators

At the beginning of the summer term I decided to extend further the children's facility in reflecting on their own performance. I knew how many of them felt about individual pieces of writing but I didn't know how they valued various pieces of writing in comparison with each other. So I asked them to choose a recent piece of writing which they were proud of.

To begin with, I gave them a list of questions:

> A piece of writing.
>
> What was its title?
> What sort of writing was it?
> Did you work on your own, or with somebody else?
> Who did you write it for?
> Who chose what it was to be?
> How did you set about writing it?
> Did you write a draft? More than one?
> What did you write it in? — a book, or paper, the computer.....
> Did you get any help with it? Who helped you?
> What do you think was good about it?
> Does it do the job it set out to do?
> Is there any way in which it could be improved?
> If you did a similar piece of writing again, would you change it in any way?

I needed to clarify the meaning of some of the questions before the children began. For instance, we talked for some time about who chooses what writing they do. We agreed that the choice could be:

- almost entirely the teacher's – for instance, 'write a haiku about an animal' (limiting the child's choice merely to choosing which animal), 'to go in a class book' (a pre-arranged audience).
- shared between the teacher and the children – for instance, 'Respond in writing in any way you like to the story I have just read to you so that your writing can be read out in assembly' gives the children more choice, but with the audience and the content still determined by the teacher.
- largely the choice of the child – for instance, where a child chooses the type of writing, its subject matter and its audience. Jenny, for example, was unable to find out whether or not the centre of the moon was hot and ended up writing to Patrick Moore to ask him.

The first evaluation of this sort that the children did was in their journals. I found that the children were divided equally between those who chose pieces of writing they had done on their own and those who chose writing they had done in collaboration with someone else. I was interested to see that the children tended to select pieces in which they had an element of choice.

> I chose what to write (Karen)
>
> Mrs. Farrow and me chose half the choice (Jenny)
>
> I chose what we wrote (Andrew)

There were some interesting responses to my question about how they set about writing:

> I set about it by doing a bit of thinking then I started to write down the story (Anna)
>
> I drafted my story first. I wrote my story out once then I read it then the bits I didn't like there I either changed them for a new word or sentence or I took it out (Karen)

Alex described how he wrote in collaboration with a friend:

> One person made up one thing and the other made up another thing. We drafted it and we wrote it in a book. We had two goes on it before we got it right.

In response to the question 'Who helped you?' Clare wrote:

> Well you corrected the spellings and you DID help me choose which story I could do next.

Other children cited, 'One of my friends', 'My mum', and in Carl's case, 'My mum and dad and sister'.

Andrew's comment about a piece of information writing he had done in collaboration with a friend is interesting. It takes for granted that this is a piece of writing produced in collaboration. The second sentence refers to a comment made by me about a previous piece of his writing and illustrates his relaxed attitude towards my observations.

> We were pleased with are swollow writing because we think we gave out a lot of ~~im~~ information and ~~we it~~ made sence. I admit that I came out in a rash of aposstrophys and commas so next time I will try not to.
>
> Who helped you with this writing? I am glad you were pleased with it, because it was good.

Responses to 'Is there any way this can be improved?' included:

> By making it a little bit longer (Martin)

Melanie showed that she was in need of some help with arranging her initial ideas:

> Next time what I would like to do is be able to put it in order because I had a lot of rubbing out so pieces about the face would fit in with the rest.

I was fascinated by these responses. I felt a sense of satisfaction when I read how clearly the children understood and took for granted the way in which they and I contributed in varying degrees to the choice of writing. I sensed the value of collaboration – how much a writer gains by writing with somebody else. And I was pleased with the confidence displayed by those who could discuss openly with anybody at school or at home the matter of selecting the next writing task.

I found, however, that the children had lost momentum by the time they reached the last four questions, having put much effort and interest into answering the ones at the beginning. So two weeks later I gave them a record sheet (see opposite) to fill in which concentrated on those questions which hadn't been answered in detail before. This produced the sort of responses I was looking for. In response to 'What I was pleased with', John wrote,

> I was pleased with the information I gave.

WRITING POLICY IN ACTION

RECORD SHEET

Title: Name:

                                                Date:

What I was pleased with:

What I'd like to do better:

What other people said:

Teachers comments:

The Writing Environment 73

Melanie wrote:

> it sounded realistic and you could imagine you were there.

Other responses included:

> I described it well (Amery)

> It made the reader think he or she is there (Daniel)

and

> because it had a real feeling (Karen)

Kristina was able to reflect upon how the ending of her description of her visit to the local church referred back to the beginning,

> when the beginning was 'I walk into a big room' and on the ending I thought it was good because at the end it says, 'walking out of the door, noise again.'

In response to 'What I'd like to do better', some of the writers were able to be more specific:

> I could do a little more about when it stands on two legs (Alan)

> I would like to add a bit more in the 8th and 2nd line (Alex)

and

> I would like to give it a bit more thinking and if I re-wrote it I'd imagine I was there before I started to write (Adam)

Some, however, were happy with what they had written:

> I don't think I can do anything better to my writing because I put all that I could remember from that wedding to the writing. I would spoil it by putting more because I would be putting stuff in that I don't know because as I told you earlier that I put in all I could remember.

This heartfelt statement of Melanie's reflects the commitment she feels for that particular piece of writing and, incidentally, demonstrates how she is experimenting with increasingly complex sentence structures.

Other people's comments are still supportive and positive, showing the ability in the responders to identify what is good about a piece of writing:

> Amery said it was good for anybody who had just got a budgie (John)

> Melanie said 'I think it was good and well described because I have never been to funeral' (Joanna)

> Anna Rooney said that it was good and and she thought it had a lot of expression and the bit about ghostly feeling Anna thought it was brilliant (Caroline)

Alex receives a hint of constructive criticism from Stuart,

> Stuart thought it would be better if I added a bit

For some time the children had been used to taping recommendations of books they had read. So I decided to extend the tape recorder's use into two other areas: writing evaluations and response partner work. I told the children that they could still carry out both of these activities if they wished but that they might record them on tape if they would rather.

Carl works out his feelings about his cinquain as he goes along:

> I didn't give a title to my cinquain because I couldn't think of one. I liked it 'cos it describes what he is doing, like falling and he ached all over when he got . . . fell at the bottom so I put hurt very much. I'd like to do it better by not just putting falling but that was the only thing I could think of then and 'It hurts very much', well, I didn't like it very much but then I did like it quite a lot.

It is clear that he is dissatisfied with one line but that on the whole he is proud of the way he has managed to encapsulate a story into five lines.

On the whole, the taped evaluations were similar in essence to the written ones, with the writers being less self-critical if anything and tending to say considerably more than they wrote. Much of what they said was of a celebratory nature. Adam's story had been acclaimed by the class and his taped comments echo his feeling of pride:

> This is a story called 'Zak and the Brave Man'. Its got the same theme as 'The Dog Who Saved the Man'. Its about . . . (here follows a resume of the story). . . . When I read it through I felt like it was a really imaginative piece of writing. . . . I thought it explained it well and it was quite good. . . . I'm quite pleased with it, no, I'm very pleased with it, to tell the truth.

Rachel's comments about the prayer she wrote for and read out in the class assembly was a breakthrough for her, since it was about the first time she had shown any confidence in herself as a writer:

> I was pleased with the last bit that said 'make us be like the dog in the story' and the bit where it said, 'Thank you for making us what we are now'. I don't think I could do anything to improve it.

I was particularly pleased with this last taped comment. I had been worried for most of the year by Rachel's low opinion of herself as a writer. I had worked hard to persuade her that the things she said in writing were valuable and worth sharing with others. She remained a very diffident writer, however, and certainly would not have ventured to write down the comment which she made on tape, if only because it would have been too laborious a task for her to do. I found the tapes added a useful dimension to the classroom, in that they gave me insights into children's perceptions which I might not have otherwise had. It also highlighted the fact that not everything worth saying has to be recorded in writing, as well as giving the children a chance to choose whichever medium they prefer.

I have already described the response partner work at the beginning of this chapter. I also found having them tape their conferences very useful to me, in helping me understand better how they worked together in this way. The tapes show the progress the children have made during the year in their understanding and appreciation of the purposes of writing and of the value of using the rich resource of each other in the process of writing.

The children have by no means yet arrived at a stage of complete confidence in evaluating their own and each other's writing. The process which has been initiated this year needs to continue. They need further experience of evaluating their own and each other's writing and they need opportunities to increase the range of writing they attempt while also increasing their knowledge of the different criteria for success in different genres. Given the atmosphere of a supportive writing community, they should in time achieve these goals.

Notes

1 *English for Ages 5 to 16*, Department of Education and Science and the Welsh Office, London, HMSO (1988).
2 *English in the National Curriculum (No. 2)*, Department of Education and Science and the Welsh Office, London, HMSO (1989), p. 29, para. 3.

4 A year's progress

> The assessment process should not determine what is to be taught and learned. It should be the servant, not the master of the curriculum. Yet it should not simply be a bolt-on addition at the end. Rather it should be an integral part of the educational process, providing both 'feedback' and 'feedforward'.[1]

Charting progress is a necessary part of the whole teaching process. Teacher's informal and formal evaluations constantly inform the kinds of intervention they make in planning classroom activities. This is just as true of writing as it is of other areas of the curriculum. Cath Farrow's class were given opportunities which led them to be able to comment on their own and other people's writing, to evaluate it in terms of its success in doing the job it was intended to do. As they identified features they were satisfied with or wanted to improve they were steadily building up their knowledge of criteria which can be used to judge successful writing in a whole variety of curriculum areas.

This chapter is about assessing progress, but it necessarily involves looking at the writing curriculum generally, since without some idea of what should be included in a full curriculum for writing it is difficult to decide what to distinguish as important for assessment and evaluation. As TGAT recommends, keeping records of progress should be part and parcel of curriculum planning. Deciding what to assess and how to carry out assessments will be central features of any school's writing policy. In Chapter 2 we looked in detail at examples of writing which might not necessarily be considered part of the traditional writing curriculum. Notes, jottings, reflective writing and drafts can reveal writers' capabilities just as much as more finished or formal pieces of writing can and so need to be taken into account when planning for a balanced writing curriculum for pupils at any stage of their schooling. But for any young writer to be able to show what he or she can do with writing the teacher also needs to make opportunities available for a variety of writing experiences and plan for the kinds of constructive intervention outlined in Chapter 3. As the first chapter emphasised, policy is made up of ideas in action. The list of what content should be included in a writing curriculum can be seen as the ideas; the classroom organization which makes it possible to carry out the curriculum forms the action.

To summarize, then, before going on to outline a framework for assessment, any policy about writing will need to take into account:

1 The different writing experiences which should be included in a full writing curriculum:

- What models of writing are offered?
- What range of purposes?
- What readers?
- What forms or formats for writing

2 What happens to writing when it is finished and how it is treated. Will it be:

- published?
- displayed?
- given away?
- put in the bin?
- responded to and redrafted?
- responded to and kept?

3 How the classroom is organized for writing. Are there:

- special places for writing?
- times for the children to choose when they will write?
- opportunities to read and comment on others' writing?
- chances to work on a piece of writing to get it right?
- examples of different kinds of text available, visible and used?

The children described in Chapter 3 gave us evidence of a policy working; they are well on the way to becoming confident and competent writers. They have grasped, clearly and firmly, the idea that they can make changes to their own writing, or approve of what they have done. They are confident in offering their early attempts, or carefully finished pieces, to others for their response, knowing that in their classroom response will be constructive. In terms of development as writers they have come far. An important part of any writer's development is the capacity to become a more self-aware reader, particularly of your own writing. As is clear from the description of what went on in the classroom, a whole series of experiences need to be planned for young writers to develop this ability. These experiences can be recorded and evaluated as part of a policy about what makes for a full and fruitful writing curriculum, but how can the children's growing abilities be described as part of an objective judgement about progress? It is difficult to capture Rachel's confidence or Adam's pride through formal or regularized assessment schedules. These increasing abilities, which certainly are part of a writer's development, need to be explained through the evidence of the children's writing itself. And this presents us with some challenges as teachers and assessors, so that two more important parts of a policy lie beneath the following questions: How do we describe what a child can do with writing? What information do we want to pass on to colleagues (or have passed on to us) as helpful records of achievement in writing?

We wanted to see just what would be possible or helpful in keeping and passing on information so we decided to look at the writing of two children throughout their year in Cath's class. In trying to track children's progress as they grow in confidence as writers and self-critical readers, we have deliberately taken the hardest path. We have chosen two children who were already technically competent writers when they came into the class. Andrew and Sally were both able to write clearly and accurately for their age (then 8) with varied and interesting vocabulary. They were capable of organizing chronological and non-chronological text and of varying writing to suit differing audiences. There would be no doubt of their competence at Key Stage 1 and levels beyond.[2] They represent the kinds of pupil who test the teacher's ingenuity in describing progress because they are already highly competent. What *did* they learn as writers during their year in Cath's class?

Different writing experiences

Looking at their writing books, which they used for early drafts and notes as well as for work towards more finished pieces, one feature is immediately clear. As time passes, both Sally and Andrew introduce more pictures and diagrams into their work, either to illustrate or to set out ideas. They move away from straightforward narrative towards a more frequent use of interesting layout. Their early drafts of stories look like the pages of story books. Their poems are laid out in varied patterns and lines. Their notes are not always arranged in lists down the page; they sometimes use flow charts, and their drafting includes the use of arrows and asterisks. All of these features suggests increasing confidence in handling a variety of forms of layout and an awareness that text can be moved about, rearranged and changed to suit what the writer wants it to do. The effect of varied reading experiences and conscious attention to format and layout has influenced the possibilities these writers have for expressing their ideas, opinions and feelings in a form which will serve them best. They are able to exercise some choice.[3]

A few examples might help make this clear. Andrew has 43 pieces of writing of different kinds in his writing books. Sally has 42. These represent not all the writing done by them during the year but a fairly representative sample. They include:

- chapters of a lengthy story
- some completed short stories
- poems in different forms including acrostics, haiku and cinquain
- drafts of letters – to an author, to some students who asked for book recommendations and to a friend who has left the school

- notes taken from a television programme about animals; notes from books about wild life
- science experiments
- draft questions and an account of an interview with the local vicar
- brainstormed ideas while listening to music
- reflective writing about likes and dislikes
- comments by other children about the writer's latest work
- regular self-chosen spellings to concentrate on and practise.

What do we do with writing?

This spread of writing suggests wide experience of models for writing as well as opportunities to write about subjects chosen by the children themselves. The readership varies from friends in the classroom, the writer herself or himself and the teacher, to friends in other places, pupils in other classes, adults known and unknown. The purposes of writing include, for example: informative writing for the guide to the local church; writing to communicate ideas and opinions to student teachers, a favourite author, others in the school; writing in preparation for non-written outcomes – school assembly and the Pandora play – to amuse, enlighten or entertain; writing to satisfy themselves as they attempt to get to grips with unfamiliar forms; and notes to remind themselves about ideas.

Some writing will be worked on again and reach published form, other pieces will have served their turn and may never be looked at again. There will be books, pamphlets, computer print-out, letters, playscripts, anthologies of reflections and poems, wall displays all demonstrating to these children that the writing they do is seriously valued and deserving of public notice. And in its publicness it will need to be edited and proof-read so as to make it as clear as possible.

Most particularly, the writing done by the children in this class is seen as a basis for the writers themselves to make evaluations of their present capabilities and the areas they would like to improve. Chapter 5 describes the process of self-evaluation in detail but here we pick up on their choices drawn from the whole year's writing.

When Sally and Andrew were asked to choose the six pieces of work they were most pleased with, Andrew decided on the following:

1 'Dr Doom's Adventures'

   I think it is a funny well written piece of writing.

2 'The Bear'

   A poem about a hibernating bear.

3 'Frankinstien'

   Frankinstien is trying to be famous!

4 'Disaster came to the world!'

> The Thurropuss (half dog half cat) saved the world.

5 Recommended book

> I added an excstreamly good drawing

6 'The magic fireworks'

> Hihgly excsplosive!!

Sally's choice was as follows:

1 Candle science

> It was about a sort of progject we did with our teacher about a kind of science and after we had done it we had to write about it.
> I liked my piece of writing because I described it quite well and people could understand it.

2 Pandora work (a theatre) (and writing)

> We did a theatre for pandora work and we tried to raise some money for the guide dogs.
> In the end we raised £8.9p and I was really pleased but it was the writing I was quite pleased with.

3 Planet writing (a letter)

> I was pleased with it because I think I discribed well and you can imagine what the planet looks like.

4 'The Apple with 400 Eyes' (a story)

> I was pleased with it because we made it short and exciting and discribed it well and not long and boring.

5 Looking at an animal (cat)

> I was pleased with it because I discribed it well.

6 Haiku (about Alice)

> I liked this Haiku because it said clearly and made it sound real.

The choices Andrew and Sally made reflect the variety of writing experiences they have had and indicate that both of them understand that writing means more than narrative. They take equal pride in informative, explanatory pieces and in imaginative writing. Their choices are drawn from writing which will be read by people outside the classroom, as well as themselves and their friends.

In describing their progress as writers during the course of the year, then, some mention must be made of the different opportunities they have had for writing, the range of purposes and the variation in readership. Young writers cannot learn to exercise choice unless they have had the opportunity to try out different kinds of writing and the experience of varied forms and formats in their reading.

In Chapter 2 we outlined our description of writing development as an increasing ability to:

1 fulfil the writer's own purposes or intentions and to choose the most suitable way of doing this;
2 take account of the needs of a reader;
3 use different forms, genres or formats for writing;
4 handle technical conventions.

Looking carefully at selected samples of writing revealed that for a full description it is necessary to take account of not only what each child can do in a given piece of writing but also how the classroom approach to writing will influence what the young writer can do or will be able to do in the future. The children in Chapter 3 have now moved on to another class with a different teacher. Chapter 3 gave the chance to look at a few snapshots of their writing experience and to see what classroom approaches they are familiar with. This is not always possible even within a school when classes change at the end of a school year and almost impossible when children move from one school to another. When we meet a new class in September it is helpful if we know something of what they can do and where they are poised for progress. If we do not, then the children are likely to suffer from our lack of knowledge. It's not so much a case of 'We've done that before' but 'We can do that; now we need experience in doing this'. However, children are not likely to feel confident enough to warn us, nor to have the foresight of what the next challenges should be. We need information if we are to plan appropriately for children to develop their writing.

Passing on information

One of the most effective ways of passing on information about what a child can do with writing is to select examples of the writing done during the course of the year. However, it would be a dedicated teacher indeed who could, or would be prepared to, read through the total yearly output in all curriculum areas of the whole class she is about to inherit! Some selection is necessary. What follows is a description of how we evolved a format for a folder of writing which need not take up a great deal of a teacher's time but would form a useful continuing record and a basis for end-of-year assessment. In Cath Farrow's class some of the selection had already been made by the children choosing their six most pleasing pieces. As we saw from Andrew and Sally's choices, these do not necessarily group round work done for 'English'. In balancing their choices we made one or two more which helped to show the range of writing capabilities for each child. To Andrew's selection we added a very brief example of his planning by using flowchart diagrams and the notes he made from the television programme about animal predators. To Sally's selection we added the 'Flying Frog' cinquain and her letter to the students giving advice on books for children.[4]

Taken together, these pieces show the varied facets of each child's writing capabilities over the year and form the centre of a useful record of their progress. But looking at pieces of writing without some sense of context leaves many questions to be asked, as we noticed in Chapter 2. What kinds of contextual information are needed if a child's writing record is to be as helpful as possible without being a massive burden either for the teacher who compiles it or for the teacher who receives it?

One of the difficulties in keeping records of achievement lies in the amount of writing which is often required for those records to give genuinely helpful information. Checklists tell us nothing, but lengthy written records run the risk of never being adequately read or noticed – dispiriting for everyone. The format which we developed involves a minimum of work for the teacher but allows for a wide range of writing to be acknowledged and included. The summarizing information drawn from the selected samples is brief and succinct but adequately reflects the individual's progress in writing over the course of a year.

Briefly, the Record of Achievement in Writing includes:

1 A list of the different kinds of writing done during each term.
2 Six pieces of writing (two per term) selected by the child, including the Writing Record Sheets compiled by the writers themselves and giving their reasons for selecting those pieces.[5]
3 Six pieces of writing (two per term) selected by the teacher and commented on in the form of the analytical framework outlined in Chapter 2.
4 A Summary Sheet compiled by the teacher at the end of the year drawing on the comments in the file as well as classroom observations.[6]

This form of recording progress in writing involves little extra effort by the teacher because it uses the expertise of both child and teacher in selecting the samples to include. A very short comment by the pupils about why they selected each piece can begin to give the reader some sense of context. Inviting children to choose the work with which they are most pleased in any one term or year gives a basis for recording their growing ability to make evaluative judgements as well as providing a chance to see just how competently they are handling the demands of making choices across a wide range of writing experiences. In the *Non-Statutory Guidance for English* provided by the National Curriculum Council, the section entitled 'Gathering Evidence of Achievements' makes the explicit point that children's evaluations should form part of continuing assessment: 'Involving children in self-assessment helps them to a better understanding of their own strengths and needs.'[7]

The children's choice of writing examples can then be balanced by the teacher's selection so that as wide a range as possible can be included. The

Non-Statutory Guidance makes the further point about the need to include a variety of writing to make a complete record:

> The recording of children's progress in writing needs to include drafts of writing as well as completed writing. It is useful to record how the child tackles writing, revises text and discusses and reflects on it. Samples of children's writing should be collected over a key stage so that development and range can be monitored. Writing is an area where children can be involved in self-assessment, discussing and commenting on their work.[8]

Although we developed the Record of Achievement in Writing before this *Guidance* was formulated, the format we suggest allows for all these points to be taken into account. The value of keeping and commenting on drafts has been made clear in Chapter 2; comparing different versions of the same piece can give invaluable information about what children can do with writing. Similarly, the Writing Record Sheet mentioned in the last chapter forms the basis for children to reflect on their own writing, to make their own assessments of the effectiveness of any given piece and, importantly, to take a hand in planning for their own progress. The folder which we recommend can be readily continued throughout a key stage and would be an ideal focus for discussions between colleagues about children's writing development. The four analytical categories offer some structure but can be used flexibly enough to avoid the framework becoming a strait-jacket.

In our suggested format for recording achievement in writing the teacher need only make detailed comments on two pieces of work for each child in a term. This means paying close attention to approximately sixty pieces of work over a period of ten or so weeks. At a rate of about six a week there should not be significant overload as each set of comments should only take a short while to write down. Further information will be needed, however, to give a fuller context. This, again, can be quite effortless – a simple listing of the kinds of writing the class has experienced during the year, in all areas of the curriculum, not just English. It needs only one list for the whole class and can be compiled termly as part of routine evaluation. Completed each term, such a list enables clearer planning for future writing. If, for example, it becomes clear that the children have had greater experience of factual writing than of imaginative or fictional writing during one term, a summary list like this will focus on the need to provide a different balance in the future.

These general descriptive sections form the basis for a rather more focused view of individual children's progress in writing and lead to the compilation of a summary at the end of the school year. Ideally, the Record of Achievement in Writing should form part of a whole language profile, including information and comments from parents, and it would be easily possible to add such a section. The format could be readily adapted or expanded to include the other Attainment Targets for English or any other area of the curriculum. The section headed 'Reporting' in the *Non-Statutory Guidance* suggests the following as a basis for deciding what information should be included in an adequate report of individual progress:

> Teachers will use the evidence, *gathered over time*, to write a summary of what children have achieved, and where support is required. Schools will decide *when* such information is reported. Information might include:
> - teacher summaries made at different times over the year;
> - children's comments made during discussion with the teacher;
> - parent's comments;
> - samples of evidence gathered by child or teacher;
> - suggestions for future learning.[9]

Most of these criteria are met by our suggested format for a Record of Achievement in Writing. Most significantly, since writing samples will be drawn from all areas of the curriculum, the folder allows for assessment and reporting to be carried out over a wider range of activities than those associated usually with 'English' or 'language' work. Our folder of work which forms the basis for the Record of Achievement in Writing already includes: a list of the different kinds of writing which the children have experienced during the year and six samples drawn from any area of the curriculum, selected by the children themselves with brief comments. As we have explained, these would, in a full folder, include completed Writing Record Sheets where the children have evaluated their own work. As a starting point for the third suggested section of the folder – the selection made by the teacher and commented on in some detail – we have taken two examples of writing from Sally and Andrew drawn from different points during the year to show how close examination of a few pieces of work can build to a cumulative record.

We took account of the fact that Andrew had included four stories, a book recommendation and a poem which arose from science work in his own selection. His writing work book did include a flow chart to represent some ideas about communications and some other science notes which he used for a poem. We wanted to select writing which was not purely narrative and to find two pieces of writing which would give a basis for comparison in order to see if we could detect features of progress in writing, so we had to ignore the flow chart and go for the poetry. First, we took a poem written by Andrew early in the year and one composed about half-way through the summer term. All the children were asked to write a poem during the autumn term after hearing and enjoying some of Michael Rosen's poetry. This activity was meant as a starting point for the children to see how everyday subjects and anecdotes can become the basis for poetry; and how they might begin to shape a poem in lines to make the most of their ideas.

Here is Andrew's first draft:

I'l tell you something ~~that~~
that happened to me
I ~~wetw~~ went to the phone
to give my ~~a~~ nan a ring.
~~a ring~~ || and I waited...
and waited // I put down the phone
~~phone~~
and I told my mum || She was not in
She told me to do it agian
~~agian~~ so I went in to the hall
~~hall~~ in a bad mood
I shouted out ~~t~~
to ~~number took in the~~
~~to~~ my mum |\ What is her
number? || shut up and phone her
~~her~~. I went to the Kitchen
~~the Kitchen~~ and I WENT
OUT ! || Shutting the door
with a great big
~~big~~ SLAM!
a few minutes later
I came back in
I said I was ~~going~~ going
for a bike ride
and my mum went

hmmm......
Come on I said
She didn't answer
So I went Out
On my.....
.... BiKE.

After discussion with the teacher and friends, Andrew decided to change some of his line organization. Then he checked his spelling and punctuation with help from the teacher. His final draft looked like this:

> I'll tell you something
> that happened to me.
> I went to the phone to give my nan a ring.
> And I waited. . . .
> and waited.
> I put down the phone
> and I told my mum
> she was not in.
> She told me to do it again
> so I went in to the hall
> in a bad mood.
> I shouted out
> to my mum
> What is her number?
> Shut up and phone her.
> I went to the kitchen
> and I WENT OUT!
> Shutting the door
> with a great big
> SLAM!
>
> a few minutes later
> I came back in.
> I said I was going
> for a bike ride
> and my mum went
>
> hmmmmm. . . .
> Come on I said
> she didn't answer
> so I went out
> on my . . .
> . . . . . Bike.

From the first version it is clear that Andrew knows that he can use writing to make his feelings known, and his drafting shows more qualities of competence. Following the analytical framework used in Chapter 2 we can say that he shows his *intentions* and the *choices* he makes by:

- selecting a particular – and dramatic – everyday incident to shape into a poem
- fulfilling the genre requirement of the task as set by the teacher.

He demonstrates his *awareness of the reader* as he:

- makes an immediate link with readers: 'I'll tell you'
- writes in an amusing way about a familiar situation which at the time was highly

emotionally charged; he knows that others can appreciate this kind of incident with the amused detachment of hindsight.

In terms of *form and organization* he:

- redrafts to present his ideas in the most effective places, using line endings and variation to emphasize points
- confidently rearranges, deletes or leaves the text alone
- has effectively used his knowledge of how other writers put texts together.

He shows his awareness of *technical conventions* as he:

- uses capitals and rows of full stops for effect
- has few problems with conventional spellings
- identifies and corrects errors with help.

But at this stage it seems sensible to add a section to indicate where Andrew needs further help. He *could work on*:

> General punctuation. Obviously he knows how to punctuate sentences, but needs to be helped to self-correct when he has missed them.

Early in his time in this class, then, Andrew was showing his overall competence as a writer. He knows that in a poem like this you can use the cadences and rhythms of natural speech to help organize the lines, that punctuation helps express tone of voice, and he has understood that the ordinary and everyday can be a basis for writing. What progress does he make? We need to look at some of his later work to answer that question.

Every now and again, Andrew writes a poem. Some are written when the whole class is working on an idea – as with the first haiku and acrostic poems – but others are self-chosen, both in terms of subject matter and form. One of the pieces of work he was most pleased with, the poem about the bear, is an example of this independence of choice. Much later in the year, two experiences led to Andrew writing in a particular way about another subject he has chosen. All the class were very interested in a television programme about animal predators and their prey. Some time before that the class had been experimenting with the form of poem known as the 'cinquain'. In his notes after watching the television, Andrew writes:

> A cheetah was after a gazzele, the gazzele dodged to defend. The cheetah was out of breath and gave up. the gazelle may knot be as fast as the cheetah. But is as cunning . . .

Later he writes this cinquain:

> cheetah
> A Carnivore
> runs swiftly to its ~~prey~~ (lunch)
> pulls it down the prey is hopeless
> Feasting!!

It is quite obvious that Andrew has exercised total choice about writing this information as a powerful and effective poem. It is, in fact, not a piece of writing associated with 'English' work but a scientific observation.

In terms of the analytical framework he makes his *intentions* and *choices* clear as he:

- fulfils his own intentions entirely by choosing an expressive form for his view of information drawn from a factual source
- has confidently completed the task.

As to *awareness of the reader*, this is a little more problematic as any poem assumes a generalized audience. He:

- has no clearly identified reader indicated in the text although he knows that anybody in the class might read it
- has achieved the most difficult task – a piece written for all. (This is what published poets do!)

The *form* and *organization* are spare and elegant as he:

- follows the cinquain form accurately
- uses its economy to make maximum impact.

And his awareness of *technical features* is shown when he:

- writes a clear and confident first draft
- spells accurately
- shows, by his editing that he has made a conscious choice about how best to express his ideas by avoiding repetition.

Little need be said by way of criticism, except that he *could work on*:

> General punctuation – still!

In looking for signs of progress, it is clear that Andrew has made some important steps forward in understanding himself as a writer. This is the first draft and apart from his alteration of the first use of 'prey' because of repetition, it comes fully formed on to the page. Looking at Andrew's poetry as one type of writing which indicates progress throughout the year it is clear that he has developed a sureness of organization and a confidence about choosing to write in a particular form. He shows that he can not only write in a way which directly involves his readers but also for a general and unknown public – a sign of a writer who knows what he can do. Technically his work is competent, although he needs still to be reminded about editing sentence endings. Just looking at two pieces give some important information about progress as well as indicating his prowess in writing in two areas of the curriculum.

Sally's poetry similarly developed to the point where she could work within given structures on subjects she had chosen. The poetry in her writing book shows that she will sometimes choose to write poetry for her own pleasure and, like Andrew, will choose to write observations of the natural world in the form of poetry. Where Andrew has included in his personal selection of pieces a poem about a hibernating bear, Sally writes poetry about a flying frog. She shows that she has a wide vocabulary and is technically very competent indeed. Her poetry reveals her capabilities in recording and reflecting on information drawn from a range of curriculum areas and her own selection of science and other notes shows that she is good at organizing short stretches of informational and non-narrative writing. Since in her own writing selection she included two pieces of work related to science, an account of making a toy theatre, a letter and a poem written because she felt like writing it – all short, succinct kinds of writing – we thought we would look at more lengthy pieces of Sally's writing to see how she handled extended narrative. Although she only selected one story in her own choice of 'best' work, she was a prolific narrative writer during the course of the year. Her main effort was a serial story which she continued over two terms! It is not possible to include that here. In order to compare two stories, one written early in the year and one later, we have had to use as the second example one which Sally selected herself in her list of the six she was most pleased with. If we were selecting 'for real' in order to complement the children's choice of work in the folder, this, of course, would not happen. For the purposes of detailed example for comparison we had no alternative but to duplicate Sally's choice here.

As she writes at some length, for the first example – a story written in November of her first term in the class – we have used two extracts, one from the beginning and the other from the end, from her 'Magic Fireworks' story:

> Once upon a time ago there was a little girl called lisa and it was her birthday the very next day. In bed she was thinking about what she would get. would she get some fireworks? It was near bonfire night, her mum might think she was to small to handle huge fireworks. Anyway she wouldn't get fireworks for a birthday present or would she?
>
> Next morning she opened all her presents and then dad came in and handed her a big hevy box, "From Grandma I think" said dad "I can reconize her handwriting".
>
> lisa eggaly opened the box then she shouted with glee "fireworks grandma sent me fireworks".

Lisa has an adventure where she falls down a hole and is imprisoned by a witch. She uses the three rockets as a power pack to zoom out of the witch's window. We pick up the story when she is back at home:

> The next night she lit the sparkler and it went so bright it was day for a whole hour. Then the next night she lit the golden rain and her mum and dad and lisa wached in amazmnt at all the gold wich came pouring out. The they became very rich and lisa really thanked her grndma really very much for those really magic fireworks. THE END

In this piece Sally shows how she has made particular *choices* to fulfil her *intentions* as she:

- tells a coherent story appropriate to the suggested title
- reflects in her writing some of the elements of books she has read where the girl is the central character, and magic and witches abound!

Her *awareness of the reader* is shown when she:

- starts in a recognized story-telling form, anticipating a readership or an audience for a told/read-aloud story
- uses questions and a colloquial register (for example repeating 'really') to invite reader participation.

Although her *form* and *organization* are not perfect, she:

- uses the content (three chosen fireworks) to shape the narrative; each is used precisely for its particular qualities
- keeps the story coherent, making the ending fit with the beginning by thanking grandma.

She shows some sophisticated use of *technical features* as she:

- can use speech punctuation accurately
- varies sentence openers
- uses the language of known story (for example, 'with glee').

And finally, some constructive suggestions as to what Sally *could work on*:

> Sally could look more carefully at the internal structure of her stories as the middle of this one (see Appendix) rather strays from a clear line, but generally she has a good foundation to build on.

Much later in the year she writes:

The apple with 400 eyes

One day two sisters called Sally & Krisy were playing in there bedroom when – suddenly*, Blu Blu Blu Blu Bluw suddenly this kind of song came out in a chinese kind of way the Apple *** started to sing "I am the apple with 400 eyes, I like to sing and I like to cry, I like to whispop day and night sooooooooooooooooooooooo I am the Apple with four hundred eyes," Sally said "Who are you"? The apple said "come out into the garden and I will tell you," They went down to the garden and the apple said "my name is pickle face and I am a big rosy apple" * "ohooh" said Sally & Krisy "why do you have allallallalllllllllllllllllllll those eyes"

Becuse they are alllllllllllll wishes" said pickle face – "Oh can we make some wishes" said the girls. "Oh yes," said pickle face. "Oh can we make one now," said Krisy "Yes" said pickle face. "Oh my," said Sally "What shall we wish Krisy?"

"But," said pickle face "you have to sing this song before you wish, this is it,":
"BANNNNANNA Lou lou lou lou lou lou lou BANNNANNA lou lou lou lou lou BANNANNA I wish to go to . . . . That's what you have to sing," Sally began "BANNNANNA lou lou lou lou lou BANN-NANNA lou lou lou lou BANNNANNA lou lou lou BANNNANNA I wish to go to the land of Mars bars . . . And then Krisy began to sing

>   BANNANNA etc . . . . To the land of Lollipops . . . . .
>   SUDDENLY lots of flashing lights came and

Here Sally has drawn a picture of lots of flashing lights. It is the end of her story. But after this she has listed her asterisked amendments:

> * a sound from the window sill
> ***which was what the sound was coming from
> * with 400 eyes.

An analysis of this later piece of work provides evidence that she has made some progress. As a now more accomplished story-maker she establishes her *intentions* by her *choices*. Sally:

- decides on a magic story with girls as central characters
- chooses to make her story funny – even zany – by selecting her preferred form, content and tone
- succeeds in writing something to amuse or entertain.

She demonstrates her *awareness of the reader* as she:

- involves the reader by humour
- shows a very keen sense of what the story would sound like if read aloud
- makes amendments to include information a reader needs to make sense of the story.

Her *form and organization* show that she:

- has an awareness of a clear overall structure – this is the first draft
- constructs a coherent line of incidents within a 'magic' genre; there is nothing extraneous in this story
- knows that stories do not need closures to make them interesting; in fact, she chooses to leave this story as a cliffhanger.

Her awareness of *technical features* has become even more competent as she:

- uses punctuation confidently and enthusiastically
- creates 'special effects' with both punctuation and language, adding humour and vitality; plays with language and sound for fun – 'whispop'
- spells and punctuates accurately overall, especially as this is a first draft; has developed her own system for revising her text.

But perhaps she *could work on*:

> Stories in a different genre. She does tend to use humour, magic and girls frequently! Will need some structured help to break new ground.

In terms of progress Sally has become a much more lively and engaging story-teller. The quirkiness of the early story, which suggests a latent sense of fun, becomes overt in the later piece where she not only uses humour within the telling of the story but in the layout and visual appeal. This later story shows particularly her understanding that stories are meant to be read, and very likely to be read aloud. Although the later piece is a first draft it follows a much clearer overall structure than the early example. There is an economy in 'The Apple with 400 Eyes' which was needed in 'The Magic Fireworks' and, most significantly, her progress in forming and organizing her story is shown by her confident closure of the second piece with no obvious 'ending'. Technically, she has made great strides. Where she was already a competent writer she has extended her repertoire of technical features to entertain the reader by emphasis and 'special effects'.

Andrew's story writing similarly showed progress. The first example, drawn from the autumn term gives little indication that he was aware of who he imagined might be reading his writing; his later story, written in May of the following year, has a punchy opening which creates atmosphere and expectation[10]. From a tentative approach to a particular kind of comic writing, Andrew becomes an assured exponent of the comic genre, using his knowledge of other texts to create a fast-moving and funny piece. Although he has made the tone his own, however, his organization of material is still a little shaky. He does show increased technical competence in using a wider range of punctuation and a more varied and adventurous vocabulary. Because of this more ambitious use of language he appears to be more erratic in his spelling than previously, but a brief analysis of the kinds of error suggest that this would be a good opportunity for him to look at the patterns in his spelling errors so that he can develop ways of dealing with them. Most impressive are the ways in which he has learned how to vary his sentence openers; his early piece has 'I' as the first word in almost every sentence. In the later piece he includes inviting openings like: 'Jake sighed . . .' and 'A wrinkly finger beckoned . . .'. Like Sally, he has begun to make use of illustration to enhance his writing. Clearly both writers have made significant progress and through this analysis of their writing it is possible to identify points where they would benefit from further help.

Making the final comments

We have given these examples of Sally's and Andrew's work from early and late in the year and from short and extended writing to show that commenting on progress need not involve a great deal of extra work and recording. Jotting down notes under the headings of the framework for analysis need not take any longer than responding to a child's piece of writing. If this is done with one or two pieces each term, preferably different kinds of writing, then the comments build to form a profile of what each child can do with writing; where they have made progress and where they need to go next. Alongside examples of chosen pieces and a list of all the writing undertaken in each term, these quite brief notes can form a highly informative profile of each child as a writer.

Summary sheets, like the completed ones on pages 143–58, compiled from the separate analyses, can give a brief but informative overview. Although they can be

> **Writing Profile**　　　**Andrew P**　　**Year 4**
>
> *Choices/intentions*
>
> Over the year Andrew has:
>
> - developed his confidence to write in different forms
> - become highly competent in shaping poems
> - experimented with humorous genres for story
> - become assured about choosing how he will write
> - enlarged his range of formats to include diagram and illustration
>
> *Awareness of reader*
>
> Andrew can:
>
> - adapt his writing to suit different readers by including relevant information and using appropriate register
> - go beyond this to write for a completely unknown 'general public'
> - decide when and how to involve readers in what he writes
> - use humour to entertain
>
> *Form/organization*
>
> Andrew has:
>
> - a clear sense of how to arrange short texts, for information, giving an opinion or expressing himself through poetry
> - developed a wide range of organizational devices – arrows, diagrams, flow charts, etc.
> - made some effective notes
>
> *Technical features*
>
> Andrew has:
>
> - developed a sound method for practising spellings
> - been consistently able to edit and revise his own work with and without help
> - shown the ability to vary sentence structure
> - demonstrated competent use of: full stops, commas, exclamation marks, question marks, apostrophes of omission and possession.
>
> *Could work on:*
>
> - different genres for writing ⎱ (see notes on
> - story structure ⎰ stories in file)
> - sentence boundary marking
> - more practice in note-making (see comments on 'Attack and Defence' notes)

compiled quite quickly from the termly sheets, they give a concise statement about the individual child's capabilities and helpful information about where she or he could go next. Quite brief, they provide an informative view of each child's

Writing Profile   **Sally W**   Year 4

Choices/intentions

Sally has shown that she can:

- write competently in a wide range of forms both when she is writing to someone else's brief or when she chooses for herself
- select content for informational and factual material and write it clearly and concisely
- write serious and comic poetry very effectively
- use humour and illustration well in extended narrative

Awareness of reader

Sally can:

- amuse, inform, entertain and persuade readers
- use an appropriate tone and register for different occasions
- select information necessary for particular readers

Form/organization

Sally has:

- particular ability in organizing factual information
- experimented with differing ways of using the same information
- developed a system for reorganizing text
- gained confidence and competence in organizing lengthy narrative (her writing book contains several chapters of a long story)

Technical features

Sally can:

- self-edit and revise independently
- use commas, full stops, exclamation marks, question marks, speech punctuation, apostrophes of omission and possession accurately and consistently
- select vocabulary effectively; invent words for particular effects; play with language to create atmosphere
- vary sentence length, openers and connectives to suit her intentions.

Could work on:

- experiments with more varied genres for extended narrative (see notes on 'The Apple with 400 Eyes')
- developing and using her obviously good ear for language
- trying out more formats for writing, developing her ability to write notes, use diagrams, etc.

capabilities. Most particularly, they give important information on where the child is poised for progress. They are the substantial evidence of a writing policy in action. This form of record-keeping reflects a good many of the aspects which a policy will cover – opportunities to write; models and examples; different forms, purposes and readers; what happens to writing when it's finished – but two aspects of writing still need attention. One, which relates to the requirements of the National Curriculum, has not appeared here. The other has arisen now and again throughout the work we have done, prompting further questions about progress. We have not made specific reference to knowledge about language in our remarks on assessment, and we have uncovered a need to pay more attention to matters of genre. To make our exploration of a writing policy complete, we look at these in the following chapter.

Notes

1 Department of Education and Science and the Welsh Office *National Curriculum Task Group on Assessment and Testing: A Report*. London, HMSO (1989), Introduction, point number 4.
2 For example, at Level 5 children should 'produce, independently, pieces of writing in which the meaning is made clear to the reader and in which organisational devices and sentence punctuation, including commas and the setting out of direct speech, are generally accurately used' (*English in the National Curriculum*, Department of Education and Science and the Welsh Office, London, HMSO (1989)). At Level 6 they should 'write in a variety of forms for a range of purposes, presenting subject matter differently to suit the needs of specified known audiences and demonstrating the ability to sustain the interest of the reader' (ibid., p. 14). Sally and Andrew have both demonstrated their ability to do all of these.
3 This contrasts with the criticisms levelled by J. R. Martin and Joan Rothery in their study of children's writing in Australia. They point out the vast majority of the texts they studied fell into the 'recount through narrative' mould which, they assert 'reflects teachers' tastes, not children's abilities'. 'What a functional approach can show teachers' in B. Couture (ed.), *Functional Approaches to Writing: Research Perspectives*, London, Frances Pinter (1986), p. 254.
4 Full examples of all these pieces are included in the Appendix.
5 This is the ideal format. The six pieces selected by Sally and Andrew do not include their Writing Record Sheets since this was an innovation developed by Cath in the summer term after most of the work which the two children finally selected for the Record of Achievement in Writing had been completed. However, Chapter 5 includes examples of completed sheets by another class and Chapter 3 gives a flavour of the kinds of comment which other members of the class made about their own work and noted on Writing Record Sheets.
6 The Appendix includes a full outline of the contents of each section of the folder of work which makes up the Record of Achievement in Writing.
7 National Curriculum Council, *English Non-Statutory Guidance*, York, NCC (1990), Section E, para. 1.4.
8 Ibid., para. 1.11.
9 Ibid., para. 2.4, original emphasis.
10 See Appendix for the two stories: 'The Magic Fireworks' and 'Frankinstien II'.

5 Children learning to think about writing

Keeping files of work and comments on what children can do with writing offers useful – and usable – evidence of individual progress. But it can provide even more than that. Children's own contributions to assessments give the teacher a chance to glimpse the working of the child's mind; to see some of the perceptions held about what makes a piece of writing 'good'; to discover what the particular young writer sees as the next thing to tackle on the path to improving her writing. Valuable insights indeed, which help in decisions about where to intervene, either with individuals or with the class, so that children can make progress with their writing. This kind of review is part and parcel of the planning necessary for a full picture of children's progress. Any well-formed programme of work will proceed on a cycle of planning, doing, reviewing and revising. It is part of the teacher's everyday (though often unrecognized) expertise to adjust plans both formally and informally in this way. Using writing as a basis for reviewing progress is a familiar approach; close attention to children's writing has always been used as a prompt to action, showing where particular problems are arising and indicating what the writer has to do to put them right. What is different now is the recognition that the writers themselves should be involved in the process towards better writing. The Record of Achievement in Writing format we suggest means that the children themselves are active partners in reflection about writing, in conversation about it and in planning and target-making for progress. Most particularly, these evaluations by the writers themselves help the teacher understand just what the children do know about writing, perhaps about its relations with reading, talking and listening. The children's comments show the extent to which they are able to use a vocabulary which allows them to make explicit what they know about language and suggests to the teacher what they might be ready to take on next as they get to grips with the structures and uses of writing.

Looking at children's knowledge about language, in this case through writing, points to a number of possibilities for extending that knowledge. Above all, asking for the children's individual comments on their writing gives them a chance, by looking back over a term's or a year's work as a whole, to see for themselves where they have come from and what they can now do with writing. It gives them the basis for beginning to develop their own views of the different ways in which texts are constructed for particular purposes; for noticing how they change their writing according to reader and genre.

In terms of a policy for writing, keeping and using cumulative records which include children's reflections is the tangible evidence against which to judge how the policy is working. It is also the point at which policy feeds back into future classroom practice – confirming that some aims have been achieved; giving the chance to revise or reschedule other aims; forming the basis for an even wider range of aims to be achieved. It is a snapshot which captures some notion of the process which has been going on, both within the individual and in the class as a community of writers and learners.

This chapter considers how conscious attention to writing – reflecting on it, evaluating and developing a vocabulary through which to comment on it – can help teachers and children make their knowledge about language explicit. This inevitably leads to issues of genre and questions about how language is organized to make meaning in different social situations and for a variety of culturally defined purposes. This includes: talking, listening and reading, as well as writing; it involves using texts which are spoken, written and read, brief or extended, in different forms, at different levels of formality, for different purposes, and for different audiences or readers. As far as writing is concerned, this would include knowledge about organization of written texts to fulfil different intentions and purposes for known and unknown readers, including the writer herself or himself. Much of this knowledge is below the level of the child's conscious attention; one of the responsibilities of teachers is to find opportunities and plan for activities which will help make that knowledge explicit. A further responsibility is to introduce children to new terminology and concepts about language. If children are to be able to reflect fully on their own language, they will need access to a vocabulary which will help them do this. However, this need not mean teaching technical terminology out of context. The key to providing children with the vocabulary they will need in order to stretch and challenge their reflections on their own language use lies in timing. It need not be a matter of waiting for some vague kind of 'vocabulary readiness', but rather of introducing the terms within a context which makes sense to the child – one where she has something on which to hang new terminology. John Richmond suggests that:

> The central principle that should guide teachers in their decisions as to the use of terminology with pupils is that the introduction of terminology must be based on some prior conceptual understanding of what the terminology refers to.[1]

As an example, very small children can easily understand ideas about rhythm from singing, clapping out and generally enjoying rhymes, patterned stories and songs. Introducing children to the vocabulary they need in order to extend their awareness of what language can do is a critical area for planning but not necessarily something different and new, and certainly not a demand for 'teaching' technical terms out of context. This is an area where a teacher's own language becomes central to the children's progress. If a teacher gradually introduces the vocabulary of reflection and evaluation within everyday classroom activities, then the children have the chance to use that language as a model and example for the terminology they might use in commenting on their own work. This can be particularly important for children who have greater confidence with oral than with written work; their spoken comments, reinforced and shared with the teacher and others in the class, can form a solid base of increasing confidence in writing. The following section describes how one teacher began to develop this kind of confidence with children who had not previously been successful writers.

'I'd like to put the sentences in order'

While Cath Farrow was using the Writing Record Sheets which children filled in themselves, so was Helen Maguire with a parallel class of 8- and 9-year-olds. Some of them had significant difficulties with reading and writing. Their confidence and achievements were not in line with their ability to talk about ideas. Helen introduced the Record Sheets as part of a planned strategy intended to help the class to build on their keenness to talk. She wanted to extend the vocabulary available to them so that they could comment more effectively on writing – their own and other people's. About once a fortnight in the first half of the summer term Helen asked the children to choose a piece of work and complete a Writing Record Sheet about it. They were encouraged to select writing from different curriculum areas. The comments which follow are drawn from maths, science, local studies, history, as well as 'English' or 'language' work.[2] One of Helen's aims was that the children should begin to develop a more 'technical' vocabulary – a language about language – so that they could make explicit what they knew about writing and what they wanted to be able to do with it. Very quickly, the children got the basic idea:

5th May	I'd like to do the ending better	
17th May	I would like to do more of the story	(Cymone)
5th May	a better beginning	(Neil)
5th May	I was pleased with the middle	(Sarah)

These early comments show that the children are becoming aware of – and using – terms which help them focus on the structure of texts. They know about the importance of making satisfactory beginnings and endings to stories; they know that the middle has to sustain interest. Importantly, they are becoming aware that they are writers who can change their own texts to make them do the job better. Sarah's comments on 17 May show a development which is even more pleasing. In answer to the question 'What were you pleased with?' she writes:

'you can have it' this is the ending

and also comments:

> I wood like to do the starting better

The opportunity for Sarah to think about the structure of her story has also given her such a close focus on her writing that she is able to select some of it for quotation. Similarly, Karen's awareness of what happens when you make changes ripens as the weeks pass to a confident statement of what she would like to do with a present piece of writing. On 5 May she notes that she was pleased with 'the way it rhymes'. In response to the question 'What would you like to do better?' she comments 'I changed the rhyme and it was funney'. By 9 June her comment about how she could improve a piece of factual writing shows a solid understanding of what she can do to make her writing communicate her ideas more effectively when she comments:

> I'd like to put the sentences in order.

Textual features and the possibilities of organizing them for yourself became accepted knowledge for these children. Similarly, they demonstrated what they already knew about elements of form and genre. Being able to select information and quote or refer to it as you write about what you read is a recognized feature of writing in academic genres. Recognizing that informational text may need diagrams, or that illustration can also be text, are important steps in understanding the structures of particular genres. Graham comments that he would like to 'draw a picture' to make his explanation clearer and Deborah says she 'would have liked to draw the spider on the web'.

One of the intentions of using the Writing Record Sheets was to encourage the children to become more attentive readers of their own writing. Sarah's quotation from her own work shows just how this process was beginning to work, and, in fact, a pattern of selection emerged across the whole class:

> I was pleased with wiht Basils putting his finger on his nose

and

> I liked it when he trow the knife at the ghost (Garry)
>
> It pleased me when I wrote about the fish medicine that could cure it (Deborah J)
>
> because in my story I keep going to the wood and finding gold (Ian)
>
> I could of given my freind and the man at the museum a name (Karen C)
>
> I would like to miss out the shouting. (Deborah A)

From the early stages where they learned to identify what they liked about their own work, after only a few weeks these children are able to comment on just *how* they could improve things. From general statements about 'making the ending better' they have moved on to be able to say how they might go about it. Examples from two children over a period of about six weeks shows just this kind of progression. Marie moves from:

> *5th May*   Title: *Odd*
> **What I was pleased with:** because I liked it
> **What I'd like to do better:** the ending

through:

> *17th May*   Title: *Story Start – Big Wood*
> **What I was pleased with:** it was good because we went in to north pole
> **What I'd like to do better:** I would like to do more of the story.

to:

> *9th June*   Title: *My Cat*
> **What I was pleased with:** when I said that when I looked at her on the photo I start crying
> **What I'd like to do better:** when she came back with blud all over her.

As she becomes more familiar with the idea of commenting on her own work and comes to understand that she can change things, Marie is able to be far more specific and attentive. This is not just because she has been given the Writing Record Sheets and asked to comment, but is a direct result of supporting talk, conversations about what the class was reading and writing and the models and examples offered by their class teacher. Clearly Marie has made progress in her ability to pay much closer attention to her work and has begun to select areas for pleasure and improvement.

Other children make other kinds of progress in being able to demonstrate their knowledge of how they can make language work for them. Neil is a more confident writer who can already give reasons for making particular choices. His progress lies in the realization that writing is more than just correct inscription; it can record and communicate:

> *5th May*   Title: *My Nike*
> **What I was pleased with:** I liked the peace of wrighting because it was hard work and I like working hard and it was long
> **What I'd like to do better:** a better beginning

> *17th May*   Title: *the villig grig [grid]*
> **What I was pleased with:** I was pleased that i got all the quesjuns right
> **What I'd like to do better:** I would of liked to of got it all right the first time

> *9th June*   Title: *My Pet Rabit*
> **What I was pleased with:** I liked it because it was sad
> **What I'd like to do better:** I would like to make it happier.

Although Neil is showing what appears to be a contradiction in his final comments, the shift from surface features to content is very clear. He is in a good position to improve the quality of his writing because he has begun to understand that writing is meant to go somewhere and do something.

Other children learned similarly important things about what matters in writing. For Cymone, gathering information allowed empathy:

> 5th May   Title: *Information on Knight*
> **What I was pleased with:** I was pleased with my knight information because it had a fealing on me that made me feal strong
>
> 9th June   Title: *Information on the Iron Age*
> **What I was pleased with:** I felt like I was an iron age person.

One of the things that Cymone knows about language is that it can invite a reader to share an experience as well as giving facts. But the informative element of writing is an important feature, too:

> I was pleased with it because it said how to look after a rabbit   (Karen G)
>
> It made sense   (Andrew)
>
> I found a lot of information   (Iain)

And being able to construct texts to interest a reader also becomes important:

> It was exciting and you always wanted to see what came next   (Clare)

Not only does this kind of reflection allow children to realize the purposes writing can serve for them, it gives them a chance to observe their own processes as they put a text together:

> 17th May   I was pleased with the way I was thinking
>
> 9th June   I liked the way I thought. I thought about the story carefully.   (Gillian)

They can begin to make distinctions between what different forms of writing can do and they can make choices. Andrew wrote about his dog and said: 'It was very hard. I'd like to write about a cat.' Graham was pleased that he 'got all the words right' in a Searchword, but comments 'I would have liked to write a poem'.

These are all important insights for the teacher and it is pleasing to see the ways in which planning for reflection and evaluation can begin to develop confidence within just a few weeks. But adopting these strategies can also be a helpful guide for future intervention. What response could, or should, a teacher make to David's apparent complacency?

> 5th May
> **What I was pleased with:** the way I made the storie up
> **What I'd like to do better:** nothing relly
>
> 9th June
> **What I was pleased with:** the story was very long
> **What I'd like to do better:** I wouldent want to do anything else to it.

Or to Karen's obvious anxiety about accuracy?

> 5th May
> **What I was pleased with:** the imformation

What I'd like to do better: look more careful

17th May
What I was pleased with: I got all the anser right
What I'd like to do better: to get my wrighting better

9th June
What I was pleased with: I only got 7 words wrong
What I'd like to do better: to write more

The examples from both David and Karen suggest that there's much more to the process of helping children make progress in writing than simply providing them with a helpful framework for comment. What the Writing Record Sheets did provide, however, was a chance for the children to air and make explicit, on the one hand, their knowledge about the way texts are or can be put together and, on the other hand, their misunderstandings, concerns and difficulties. If David has laboured hard and long over a piece of writing, we can well understand that the idea of revising or improving it is too much for him! Karen is at least moving towards a positive way of looking at her worries and difficulties about surface feature correctness. And, of course, it is important to get the technical features right. What these last two examples show is the value of providing an environment which can challenge children to look critically at their own writing at the same time as supporting their attempts at improving their standards. They highlight the need for a policy to take account of *how* writing is tackled as well as outlining what kinds of writing children should experience.

These elements of a writing policy became crucially important when considering the need for children to be more conscious and adept at working within particular genres, organizing texts specifically for particular purposes. In her article 'Writing in Schools'[3] Frances Christie comments that 'learning how to mean' involves certain implications:

- Students in the process of learning content must manipulate different ways of constructing and organizing meaning in texts.
- Teachers must recognize the linguistic demands associated with content areas of schooling, so that they may guide students more usefully in their schooling.

This sounds like a tough agenda, if we are to know the linguistic demands of every kind of text in all areas of the curriculum. In fact, it is made much clearer if teachers build their own confidence in their knowledge about written language by paying close attention to the way children construct texts. It also becomes much easier if children, too, are encouraged from the very outset of their writing to notice how they organize texts, to reflect on that organization and to be able to reorganize their writing when they choose. Alongside this, the teacher's introduction of different models and examples and the children's expectations that they can and will examine the way established writers have put texts together, will make it easier to fulfil what Christie suggests is necessary: 'Learning to write in science, social studies, or literary studies is a matter of learning to distinguish the different generic structures associated with each field.'[4]

If teachers increase their own awareness of text organization by conscious attention both to children's writing and the reading matter which they introduce in class; if children are given the opportunity to begin to distinguish in their own writing between the elements which they think will do the particular job they set out to do and those parts which need improvement, both teachers and pupils will have a strong basis on which to build. The Writing Record Sheets from Helen's class indicate just how valuable a simple, quick format can be in encouraging children's explicit expression of their perceptions and knowledge of how writing can make meaning. Planning steadily to increase children's awareness of how to arrange language in different ways to do different jobs means creating a classroom environment which is rich in models and examples of a wide variety of texts, both spoken and written; and providing suitable structures and strategies to help reflect on those texts.

The importance of genre

The (now explicitly recognized) importance of providing children with a wide range of reading material and opportunities to write in a variety of forms and formats, coupled with the emphasis on reflecting on the process of putting texts together, has led to a much wider debate about genre. Some of the questions raised are:

- Just what generic categories of writing should children be exposed to?
- What genre forms should children be able to use?
- At what stage in their education?
- How should these genres be taught?

This recent interest in genre and the development of children's writing has led to a concern about the predominance of narrative (or recount of experience) as the (apparently) preferred written form used by children in primary schools and fostered by teachers. In the early years this often takes the form of daily 'news' writing, some teachers will use the word 'story' to mean any kind of writing. The suggestion is that teachers should be more conscious of different kinds of text and actively create chances for children to work with a variety of structures. In order to do this, teachers themselves need to have greater familiarity with generic structures. J. R. Martin's work in Australia has revealed that:

> In spite of the fact that Narrative is the main type of writing encouraged by schools, and that the vast majority of writing in primary school tends in this direction, only a minority of children learn to write successful narrative by the end of Year 6. Poor writers learn use of Observation/(Comment) or Recount genres; and average writers often produce Narratives lacking in the development of crucial stages. Teachers do not really understand what is wrong and so cannot help.[5]

Martin and his colleague, Joan Rothery, use the idea of genre in a rather wider sense than we may expect. It is intended to include not only literary uses of 'genre' – for example, mystery stories, narrative poetry, soap operas – but also the 'staged purposeful processes through which a culture is realized in language'. This means that they pay attention to both the process of writing and the product of that writing; the social and cultural expectations associated with particular forms of writing; the registers (or levels of formality) involved in particular forms of writing. This relates very closely to the description of knowledge about language in the Cox Report where stress is laid on both the cultural and linguistic aspects of genre and reflects the comments made in Chapter 1 of this book about the essentially cultural base of all language capabilities.[6]

In criticizing Australian curriculum statements, Martin explains that 'these documents argue that children should write in a variety of forms for a variety of purposes'. But not only are these lists open-ended and not only is no guidance given about the relative importance of some forms or functions above others, they are not informed by a theory of writing development. He raises a number of questions; for instance:

> Is each form tied up with one major purpose, or are form and purpose independent? How do stories differ in structure and content from reports?[7]

In a later article, with Joan Rothery, the argument is followed up by specific suggestions about how teachers can best contribute to the development of children's writing:

> One important role is that of organizing students' writing processes. Children need to be given opportunities both to write and rewrite, and they need a chance to interact with their teachers and peers in this process. Another role for teachers is that of evaluating student writing. We do not intend this in the traditional sense of someone who grades and corrects; rather, we mean that teachers must evaluate the stages children are at in developing skill at a genre . . . Finally teachers must actually TEACH writing by intervening, positively and constructively, with respect for the child's text.[8]

There are some difficulties about the suggestion that there are 'stages' as children develop 'skill at a genre'. It seems that Martin and Rothery accept a view of learning as consisting of gathering separate 'skills' which are then strung together to make competence – in this case in writing in different genres. It is now quite clear that children's capabilities to work within different generic forms depend to a very great extent on the opportunities they have been offered to read, talk about and try out a wide variety of types of written texts. Further to that, and most importantly, it is now widely recognized that children's learning consists not of putting together different 'skills' but of a gradual consolidation of experiences, practice and techniques which are visited and revisited throughout their schooling. Indeed, as far as writing is concerned, it is questionable, and open to argument, whether any adult writer can ever claim to have got to grips with all the 'skills' necessary for writing in a wide range of genres. It seems that even mature writers continue to learn and develop their expertise!

Another problem associated with the notion of teaching generic forms lies partly within just what can be defined as a genre and, in turn, has implications for the compilation of a writing curriculum. As Bruner pointed out, it is probably more helpful to understand genre as both descriptive of a way of categorizing forms and formats for writing and a way of organizing knowledge and experience. To suggest that there is a catalogue of genres which can be introduced, practised and perfected, could lead to the worst kind of checklist approach to teaching writing. Continuing from Bruner's useful definition, it would be more helpful, perhaps, to view genre in a more flexible way. In his book *The Double Perspective*, David Bleich outlines the view that 'any one genre has been made up of a variety of others'.[9] He gives the television spot, women's magazines and slave narratives as examples of texts which are made up of a combination of a general category and a particular, historically developed form. Quoting Ralph Cohen, he points out that 'genre-naming fixes what is necessarily unfixable', warning of the dangers of too inflexible a view of generic categories. However, since some kind of naming is necessary if we are to be able to talk sensibly about different kinds of text, then it is as well to remember that 'genre naming or grouping is both necessary and loose.'[10]

Although it is unclear just what position Martin and Rothery take about the clear classification of genre forms, their advice to teachers reflects the current need for teachers to identify and recognize their own knowledge about language and to use this in understanding what children can do in writing: 'Teachers can help young writers by learning to distinguish the genres their pupils are writing in and noting the kind of language used to realize each.'[11] Their suggestion that teachers should pay close attention to what their pupils write to detect features of competence rather than simply to identify faults is particularly helpful. Later, Martin and Rothery argue more broadly that children need to develop their writing 'in the ways most meaningful to them':

> When teachers interact with young writers ... drawing upon both their conscious and unconscious knowledge of how language works to do so, they will, in fact, be teaching writing. Writing, like speaking, is first and foremost a way of making meaning in a context. What schools should be doing is providing children with interactive contexts in which this act of making meaning will be worthwhile.[12]

This echoes a point made strenuously by Janet White in her evaluation of the work of the National Writing Project:

> Finding enlightened ways of involving children in the process of writing is one part of developing their competence as writers, and the demonstrable benefits of this are not in question. Equal thought needs to be given to the nature of what is produced: what is it that makes, say, explanation different from speculation/reflection/ description/narration/argumentation, and when is one rather than another of these genres most appropriate? Instead of making an endless list of the functions that writing might serve in education, is it possible to identify those crucial to success in related disciplines? Children need to know how and when to choose from a range of

different types of text; such knowledge is not acquired by osmosis, but by careful guidance and intervention on the part of skilled teachers.[13]

The teachers' and children's work in this book has arisen from the combination of 'interactive contexts' and 'teaching writing' which Martin and Rothery make their focal point. The approaches described help in beginning to consider just what might be implied by the kinds of 'intervention on the part of skilled teachers' which Janet White identifies as so important to children's success as writers and learners.

We have suggested that an essential part of any policy for writing lies in the teacher's understanding of what children bring from their home cultures, their own language and literacy experiences, and in building on that awareness by creating structures which will lead to progress. The intermingling of these experiences and the new learning opportunities offered in the classroom make the dynamic which moves writing – and learning – on. The approach taken towards children's efforts, the responses given and the evaluations made, are based on a theory of cognitive development which emphasizes that what a child can do with help today, she can do alone tomorrow. Further, that theory points to the necessity of collaboration if language is fully to be developed as the central means of learning in all curriculum areas. And after the writing has been done, we have argued that it isn't enough to leave it there. Both teachers and children need to pay attention to just how texts have been put together; how they can be reorganized, if necessary, to do the job better; and what other models and examples are available for a developing understanding of genre. All of these mean a growing knowledge about language which draws out the child's implicit understanding and builds on it to extend and broaden both the knowledge and the vocabulary available to express that knowledge.

Knowledge about language can be identified not only by an individual's ability to *talk* about language, but also by the ability to *produce* language in different forms, both in speaking and writing. In order to increase children's knowledge about language, then, teachers will need to be able to help them distinguish between different kinds of texts or genres, written or spoken, to recognize their features and to be able to describe those features in a suitable vocabulary. Young writers will also need to have opportunities to decide when they want to use these different genres for their own purposes and intentions. Talking about them will help children recognize and use the characteristics of different genres which they hold as implicit or explicit literacy knowledge through experience of a variety of texts met in a variety of contexts.

As Martin and Rothery and Janet White point out, teachers need to be confident about ways of helping children to learn 'how and when to choose from a range of different types of text' to fulfil their own intentions in writing. Chapter 2 suggested a framework for identifying features in a variety of written texts which might be used to describe progress. Chapter 3 sketched some of the ways in which the classroom approach and teacher intervention create conditions which help children learn how to use their knowledge of constructing texts. The suggestions for observing and monitoring progress in Chapter 4 lead to an approach to writing which pays attention to children's growing ability to discriminate the different ways in which they might wish to use material according to the occasion and their intentions. As a way of drawing together these elements of an effective writing policy, which is, of course, a working writing curriculum, we move full circle and look again at examples of writing by some of the children whose writing we looked at closely in Chapter 2 – Steven, Oliver, Zoe, Katherine and others in their class. However, these extracts are not from their final year in the Junior School as the earlier examples are, but from their second year, where they were just being introduced to some of the ideas which led to their later confidence and competence. Their experiences highlight the value which writing can have for teachers, too, as an invaluable form of 'guidance and intervention' towards progress.

A circular argument?

Language is necessarily social and interactive and it is now widely recognized that the development of language is supported by conversation, collaboration and co-operation. How can these insights about the communality of language be used to support development in writing which is often seen as a solitary activity? Even if writers collaborate there is something essentially personal about the act of writing which seems to be at odds with what we know about partnerships for learning. If we accept that reflection on language helps us recognize what we know, how can those understandings combine with the interactive nature of language? There seem to be some paradoxes here. Reflection and the act of writing are often solitary; dialogue and exchanges of view depend on response. Perhaps a way of resolving this apparent opposition is to see writing as a dialogue of sorts, often a dialogue with others in the act of communicating ideas, but also a dialogue with oneself. One highly successful way of using the dialogic nature of writing as an effective way to reflect on language is to use a response journal where the child and the teacher correspond, or have written conversations about the work which is going on. Journals can and have been used in a variety of ways to support learning in different areas of the curriculum and sometimes controversy or concern surrounds their use.[14] If they are introduced as private journals to be read by the teacher only when the writer offers the writing to be read, questions arise such as: How much privacy should we give the writer? Will the children take advantage of the opportunity to write 'privately'? What happens if we read something which, as responsible teachers, we feel we ought to report to someone else? How do we negotiate these areas of discretion? If the journal is introduced as a work log to be responded to, how is the time to be found? These are sensitive areas and deserve fuller consideration than we can give them here.[15]

In the case of Class Two, their teacher, Belinda Kerfoot-Roberts, decided to use journals specifically as work logs. Rather than using the idea of journals in the most personal and private sense, she decided to use the idea of a journal as a working journal – as, indeed, many scientists, artists and writers have done. The difference here would be that the children's journal entries would form the basis of a dialogue with her. She wanted them to give her a chance to have the conversations with the children which she did not have time for in the ordinary course of a busy day. She saw them as an important means of teaching and recognized that they would take time to respond to fully. It was hard work. The products and by-products of the activity are evident not only from the entries but from the view we have of some of the class as writers two years later.[16] Reflective writing as it appears in the working journals allows children to experience a range of reasons for writing: to give shape to ideas, capture thoughts, develop hypotheses, ask questions; to record, select, categorize information, and to communicate ideas to a known reader. All of these reasons for writing help the children develop a sense of what it is to be a writer who can fulfil her or his own intentions, and can shape writing to suit chosen ends, for reflection and communication, for personal reading and for others to read.

In looking at what the children wrote in their journals, one of the most striking features is the way the children assume that all the language activities – reading, writing, talking and listening – are related and part of every aspect of their learning. Another important feature, as far as writing and genre are concerned, is the readiness with which the children comment on their reading tastes and preferences. The information needed to shape a text in a specific form is necessarily drawn from the texts children read and are offered as models. Since awareness and a critical approach to other texts is an essential part of understanding different generic structures, these comments from 8- and 9-year-old children give us a clear indication of their capacity for genre awareness very early on in their schooling. But, as we have already noted, this needs to be prompted and fostered by the teacher as this written exchange shows. Philip writes:

> I don't read alout because I get board of my books and I dont find my library books not very interesting because I dont enjoey reading I like it when you read but I am not very good at reading to my mum and I get board I would like more adventure books

His teacher replies:

> It's a shame you don't read a lot, Philip, as reading can be great fun and put you in adventures you could never be in real life. I'm sure if you looked you could find some good adventure books in the library. Perhaps the other children in the class can suggest books they've read.
>
> You might find it more interesting to try to read to your Mum like I read to you, giving the characters different voices. Try it, and tell me how you do.

Through this written conversation, the teacher can see that although Philip finds reading aloud painful, he nevertheless has a good understanding of what he would *like* to read. This gives her the chance to give explicit teaching ideas about how he might be able to improve his enjoyment.

In a similar way she can give a prompt to further thinking about reading tastes. Lee writes:

> This week we have been having a Roald Dahl week we have done a display of his book and we have had the magic finger, dirty beasts, Revolting Rhymes, and Geoges Mavelous Medicen I have decided that Roald Dahl is my favourite Aurther

Belinda responds:

> I'm so happy you've enjoyed Roald Dahl so much, I have too. I think we'll have another author's week later in the term – have you any suggestions of books we could read?

Lee replies:

> I do have a suggestion about another aurthers week Ursula Moray Williams the book is called Jeffy the burglar's cat

One of the noticeable aspects of this exchange is the way in which Lee shows an awareness that book titles often have capital letters, as do authors' names. His observations extend to the point where in his second entry he accurately transcribes the apostrophe in the book title.

This kind of conscious attention to detail about authors was further encouraged when the children themselves teamed up to write and illustrate books. As Sophie explains:

> I liked to do the story and picture. Me Isabel and Susan were thinking of a story and the story was the little girl Hho found the squrile. its a good story. Isable was the writer and me and Susan done the drawring we have neley finised now.

In this brief extract Sophie shows an understanding of the process of collaborative story-making and that she is prepared to make a comment on the quality of what they have done.

Belinda replied using the term 'illustration' to reinforce the availability of a specific technical term as she does in her reply to Steven. Where he writes 'story' and 'picture' she uses other words. Steven shows that he can make choices about what he wants to write and in talking through his journal he demonstrates his ability to write in a way which involves the reader when he notes:

> This week I enjoyed the story and picture. Katharine and I have riten a poem about a . . . . . you will find out. As usual can we do some more?

Belinda replies:

> I'm glad you enjoyed the author and illustrator work so much, I thoroughly enjoyed reading your story 'Poor Pig'. The illustrations were super. Of course we can do some more work like this . . . as usual!

The teacher's reply not only supplies useful vocabulary – a language with which to talk about about language – but also acknowledges Steven's humour and capability to use a repeated full stop as a 'trail' – a sophisticated device for an 8-year-old.

Other children's comments gave her further chances to 'teach by written conversation'. She is able to comment on the content of the writing, too. Mark is working with James and he comments that in their book 'James keeps blowing things up'. Belinda replies:

> Your story did seem a bit destructive when I read it, with everyone being blown up. I hope your illustrations won't be too horrific.

And although James has some difficulties with accurate spelling, he nevertheless shows that he has learned the vocabulary associated with the activity and is enthusiastic about other forms of language work, too:

> I have enjoyed doing the pitchures and ilusrashuns storys. Gareth Owens poems are good and I have enjoyed lisening to them because they are funny and they rime.

Clearly James is building his technical vocabulary by hearing his teacher use the terms 'illustration' and 'rhyme', as his insecure spelling of them indicates.

The links between reading, writing, talking and listening are made clearly when the children comment on the talks which each of them, or pairs of pupils, do for the class. James comments:

> The talk on Thursday was good and I think it was a good idear doing talks.

which gives Belinda the chance to reply:

> I thought Zoe and Linsey's talk was good, too. They had done an awful lot of research. I hope yours and Jay's talk goes as well.

thus introducing 'research' as new vocabulary about reading for information. One talk made a particular impact, with many of the class choosing to comment on it. Michaela writes:

> Euan and Owen did a talk on refrance books I realy liked it.

And Sophie remembers it in great detail:

> On Thursday we went down to the Library because Owen and Euan had a talk about books. We talked about the reference books index. there is a box in the Library. So that if you won't a book and can not find it you have to look under sport. then when you have fond it you have to look under the one you where looking for. you look for the nummber under it. if it sayes a nummber you look for the nummber and you will read it.

The children are taking in, rehearsing and showing knowledge of the differences between a variety of texts – written, read and spoken. Importantly, however, the journals gave Belinda a chance to teach about strategies for writing which support the children's efforts to make meaning. Steven writes:

> This week I liked the idea of the Playses I have been to. I mean I thought it was fun to try and rember all the playses we have been to and seeing what it remined us of. And then writing about it.

Belinda takes this as an opportunity to extend his knowledge and prompt further thought:

> I'm pleased you liked the idea of brainstorming Steven. I think we will do it again in the near future to think of another title on a different subject. Did you enjoy having the freedom to choose how you wrote about your title in a poem, story, letter etc.?

To which he replies 'Yes I did.' which reminds us of his readiness in the Fourth Year to hold a written conversation with his teacher (see Chapter 2).

As a summary of the value of this kind of reflective writing and the chances it gives the teacher to intervene 'positively and constructively' to help children improve their writing, we look at the work logs of two writers in some detail. Katherine and Oliver were two of the writers who allowed us to use their work for the text analysis in Chapter 2. In an attempt to revisit the important notion of continuity in approaches to writing, we want to emphasize the value of a shared writing policy and agreements between teacher colleagues on fundamental principles about writing. These negotiations can mean all the difference between children becoming confident and competent writers or being shackled by unclear or opposing approaches to language within a school. As we noted in Chapter 2, these children were capable writers who understood a great deal about genre and who were demonstrating implicit knowledge about language of a particularly sophisticated kind. One of the key factors which contributed to this steady progress towards competence must have been the shared approach by the teachers in the school about just what a writing policy in action should entail.

'When we put our own ideas into action'

Oliver's log is a record of enthusiasms, many of them about language work, and certainly reflects his wide-ranging interest in texts of all kinds:

> *30th January*: On Monday we started to read Georges marvellous medicine. I liked it very much.
>
> *6th February*: I liked Zig-Zag on Monday abouat eskimo's I liked the zedna story best . . . . . on thursday the last thing I did was draw my Roald Dahl poster I think that was the best thing I did all week.
>
> *23rd February*: . . . I just could not wate to do the Eskimo drama . . .
>
> *6th March*: . . . . what programs are we having next after the Eskimo program. The haiku poam's were very good.
>
> *13th March*: Ben said he did not want to do the drawing on the author and illustrator work so I have started to do the drawing on it. . . . On the places I have been to work I did not no which one to pick because there were so many places I have been to but in the end I picked Spain but I still have to wright a letter in my red book. I really do

like the Gareth Owen poems but I do not no if I want to do it with Owen [his friend] or do it on myself. But I can't wait until Gareth Owen comes in.

2nd April: I enjoyed the talk on policmen. [a talk given by two of the girls] I really did like those hats the policmen wear. When I saw Gareth Owen I thought that he was going to be young.

22nd May: The Joan Aiken books are brilliant I enjood the book called past eight o clock very much. I can't wait till we have read all of the kitchen warries. The topic books I liked out of the topic book i think that the bones were the best.

In the course of a few months, Oliver records his awareness and appreciation of visual text, drama, television, various fiction writers, poetry and poets, factual writing and talk. All of this is interspersed between comments on all sorts of other aspects of his work during a week in school. What his log clearly shows is the broad base of reading and writing opportunities which this class experienced, besides the chance for him to reflect on his work in writing. The important principle of encouraging the child's own voice and supporting what he or she *can* do allowed Oliver to mature into a writer who can tackle the demands of a wide range of writing tasks.

Katherine's process of development takes a rather different path. In Chapter 2 it was clear that she could operate very competently in a range of genres. Her work log gives us an interesting insight into her progress towards a broad range of competence:

26th January: I would also like to do more english not storys but stride ahead work and into english. I like these because there not as long as storys.

30th January: I would like to do more about a certain athor like Enid Blyton or Micheal Bond more often because i really enjoyed doing about it. Sometimes i would like to do some reading inbetween lessons becaus at home I am normally very busy. I would like to have a bit more homework though because it keeps me out of trouble.

6th February: I very much enjoyed the class talks as well and I would like to know whether we would be doing another class talk each or not.

23rd February: I enjoy Zig Zag as well because it shows the things on films . . . I liked the idea very much of having a handwriting lesson every month. When you wrote in this book you asked me whether Nicola and I have decided how to do our talk. it should be ready in about two weeks, I am very much looking forward to it.

6th March: I also enjoyed doing the haiku poems. I kept on thinking of lines but they didn't have enough silabals in them. I also enjoyed doing the illistraiting and writting well I've enjoyed it so far.

13th March: I very much enjoyed doing the places I have been to work because of the way we did it. It sort of had a flow to it. I thought that doing Gareth Owen's poems but from a different point of view was a very good idea and am looking forward to Monday when we can put our own ideas into action.

2nd April: I enjoyed very much doing our class talk. I think that the rest of the class did as well. But what I would like to know is are we going to have another round. I also liked very much Gareth Owen coming to our school. He did not look at all like what i thought.

10th April: I think that we learnt about the Eskimos more because we actually had a go at an Eskimo life of our own. Through drama the television programs and having a go at making the models look just like they would in real life. Altogether I learnt a lot about the Eskimos and enjoyed it.

We haven't any more entries that year from Katherine's journal, but I think the extracts here show very clearly just what progress can mean. She demonstrates her understanding about how language works by her comments on haiku and brainstorming 'because of the way we did it'; she shows her grasp of particular text forms and the ways they can be manipulated to suit the writer's intentions. She has already become enthusiastic about talks, laying the foundations for her full and explicit notes for a talk which we saw in Chapter 2. She also knows that talk, reading and writing can support learning; there could not be a more succinct explanation of active, participatory learning than her entry on 10 April. What happened to her urge to do exercises in English as she requested in January? As she puts it herself, she found that combining new learning with existing experience and putting it into practice is the better way to get a grip on what language and writing can do. In terms of a policy for writing we can't do better than use Katherine's words:

I am looking forward to Monday when we can put our own ideas into action!

Notes

1 J. Richmond, 'What do we mean by knowledge about L. language?' in *The North Circular: the Magazine of the North London Consortium*, London, Language in the National Curriculum Project (1990), p. 9.
2 See Chapter Three (p.?) for format of Writing Record Sheet.
3 F. Christie, 'Writing in schools: generic structures as ways of meaning' in B. Couture (ed.), *Functional Approaches to Writing: research perspectives*, London, Frances Pinter (1986), p. 224.
4 Ibid.
5 J. R. Martin, 'Types of writing in infant and primary school' in *Proceedings of Macarthur Institute of Higher Education Reading Language Symposium 5: Reading, Writing and Spelling – 1984*, p. 6.
6 *English for Ages 5 to 16*, Department of Education and Science and the Welsh Office, London, HMSO 1988.
7 Ibid, p. 14.
8 J. R. Martin, and J. Rothery, 'What a functional approach to the writing task can show teachers about "good writing" in Couture, *Functional Approaches to Writing*, p. 262.
9 D. Bleich, *The Double Perspective: language, literacy, and social relations*, Oxford, Oxford University Press (1988), p. 116.
10 Ibid. quoting R. Cohen, 'The autobiography of a critical problem', lecture presented at an annual meeting of the Midwest Modern Language Association, Bloomington,

Indiana, 4 November 1984, p. 6. A similar caveat can be found in the succinct critique of Martin and Rothery's views in Wayne Sawyer, Anthony Adams and Ken Watson (eds), *English Teaching from A–Z*, Milton Keynes, Open University Press (1988), p. 70. A more fruitful way of examining genre forms may lie in looking at Foucault's analysis of historically developed structures of discourse.

11 Martin and Rothery, p. 260
12 Ibid.
13 Janet White in the (unpublished) evaluation of the National Writing Project, School Curriculum Development Committee (1988).
14 See Nelson/National Writing Project, *Writing and Learning*, Kingston, Nelson (1989), particularly the section 'Reflecting and Responding'.
15 See work by Somerset/Wiltshire 'Write to Learn' Projects, for Example. B. Joslin and R. Whitewick, ' "First of all I didn't think the idea would work at all – an experiment in using Response Partners and Response Partner Writing" ' (1989). A range of publications, including work on reflective writing with infants, is available from The Somerset Education Centre, Park Road, Bridgwater, Somerset, TA6 7HS.
16 In keeping with respect for the personal nature of these journals, we are grateful to the children for their permission to use these extracts.

6 Conclusion: putting the policy together

The teachers whose work and classes have been described in this book were in the process of hammering out a writing policy. They began not by writing it all down as a document but by making changes to their classroom practice. They are still doing that; still asking themselves questions, still developing new ways to help their children become more effective writers. Some of them have moved to other schools and have carried their insights with them, blending their ideas with the views of new and different colleagues. They have found, as many teachers do, that such factors as the geographical area (town or country), the kind of school (small primary or large junior), and the school population (ethnically mixed or apparently monoglot) make very little difference to the kinds of question they still want to ask about writing in classrooms. Whether in the North or South of England, in a remote area or in an inner city, the concerns and preoccupations of teachers are much the same. Although this book has presented a picture of teachers in one school working on their policy for writing and much will have changed within the school by the time this book is read, experience elsewhere convinces us that the process of policy-making at Burnham Copse has relevance for other teachers in other schools.[1] This chapter aims to summarize the issues which have been raised through the process of developing a writing policy in action.

Although the separate chapters of this book have presented ideas separately and consecutively, in fact the work was going on with several classes at the same time. For three or four years the teachers had been working together to develop their ideas about writing and had made some significant strides in finding differing purposes and audiences for writing; in encouraging fluency in writing through journal keeping; and in using writing in a variety of ways to support work in all areas of the curriculum. The work documented in this book took place because of these foundations. Having found that children's standards improved over a period of time when their writing was approached differently, the next move was to try to establish a means of embedding these insights into usual classroom practice. In this way – the most successful way of developing policy –

the actions came before the detailed written formulation of policy. While we were focusing on the writing of Sue Phillips's class in order to develop a way of describing progress, Cath Farrow and Helen Maguire were putting themselves under the microscope, carefully noting the kinds of intervention they made when discussing writing with children and setting up strategies by which children could become more attentive and critical readers of their own work. For Helen this meant, particularly, finding ways to support less confident writers. At the same time, other teachers were concentrating on their cross-curricular approach, particularly using the microcomputer.[2]

So it was not a neatly parcelled experience. It spread over several years, although the work we have written about took place during one year in this developing history. Perhaps the most important point to make about the creation and formulation of a policy for writing – or for any other area of the curriculum for that matter – is that it takes time to evolve and mature. If the policy is genuinely to reflect the established good practice of teachers in the school and to continue to stimulate and challenge them and their colleagues, it will need to be worked out over time. It will also be the result of a series of discussions, negotiations and contributions by all members of staff. Although groups of colleagues often need someone to spur them on, to encourage their efforts, to pose challenges and offer the support necessary for them to meet those challenges, it is always the slowly and collaboratively devised policies which result in real and lasting changes in classroom practices.[3] As we mentioned at the beginning, a writing policy should reflect active, daily practice. Only in this way can it adequately describe and stimulate those classroom approaches to writing which will foster genuine learning.

Because a policy needs to capture daily practice, it ought also to be a useful summary of what goes on and a document capable of change and modification. In other words, it needs to be continually extended and built up without becoming too unwieldy. For this reason, the outline policy suggested here consists of a set of headings including questions and suggested strategies rather than pious and possibly unattainable abstract statements repeating the word 'should' with frightening frequency! Its form is more likely to be a set of separate, reproducible sheets than a sheaf of closely typed text and it might well be accompanied by files of plastic sleeves showing examples of children's writing to illustrate different points. Part of the policy, certainly as any particular area is being developed, might be seen as a diagram on the staffroom wall which is added to as discussions progress. It need not follow any set sequence, but is more likely to deal with issues which are most relevant to the circumstances of the particular school. Some colleagues may be confident about finding various readers for writing but want to explore ways of encouraging note making and planning; others may have found that working with word processors has helped less confident writers and want to move those insights into writing without the micro. Each school will have its own agenda.[4] The section headings which follow summarize the stages of policy-making. They should not be seen as hard and fast directions for a successful policy, rather as a series of guidelines as to the possible route to take when working through ideas.

Start by talking

If a policy is to mirror the needs and experience of both teachers and pupils, it is important to establish at the outset just which aspects of children's writing colleagues consider most important. There have been two underlying threads to the work described in this book: an awareness that teachers' own questions and activities will form the basis of any policy, although sharing ideas and offering a chance for debate and disagreement will help; and a confidence that teachers have a fund of often untapped or unrecognized expertise which needs to be acknowledged and made more public through discussion.

Early and general discussions are essential in order to begin developing a way of talking with others about writing. Although in any school there may have been a great deal of emphasis on language, on monitoring and assessing it, discussions may not have been wide-ranging enough for colleagues to discover that what one person describes as 'drafting' is another's 'rough copy'; that the teacher who confidently asserts that 'all my children are used to redrafting their work' may only mean that, just as in ages past, the children in that classroom write, have their writing corrected by the teacher, then copy it out tidily. It takes a little time to unravel just what people do mean; and time is valuably spent if it can lead to a shared vocabulary through which to talk about writing. Similarly, it may take time for colleagues to be able to describe just what they do that works well. Because teachers spend a great deal of time in their own classrooms and don't have enough opportunities to work alongside others, there is a tendency to assume that everyone works in the same way. What this can often mean is that a teacher doesn't bother to explain a really good idea or part of her classroom practice because she thinks that it 'isn't news'.

Through making clear those questions which are niggling at the back of their minds and at the same time describing ways they have found to help children become more successful writers, a group of colleagues will begin to find the common ground for mapping out the first moves on the journey towards a more formulated policy. The itinerary may begin, then:

What is important about children's writing?

- about the writing itself?
- about how we respond to writing?
- about the classroom conditions to support writing?
- about the opportunities offered to help children get better at writing?
- about the kinds of writing we value most?
- about the different kinds of writing used throughout the curriculum?

Considering *what* is important begins to sketch out the aims for a possible curriculum for writing. This will inevitably lead to the two other important elements of any writing policy – *how* the aims are put into practice, or the curriculum content, and *why* these things are important – the principles underlying the aims and the practice of the policy.

Discussions which focus on 'why' will help make explicit the implicit theories of writing and learning which are at the basis of classroom practice. For example, in discussing the kinds of writing which are given most value in the classroom, some colleagues may find that they do, in fact, give importance and status to children's tentative first attempts. This view signals very clearly a theory which is built on an understanding that writing is, in itself, a form of learning – a way of shaping ideas into a manageable and understandable pattern. Teachers who take this view will probably also set up an environment which encourages children to use and develop their own language resources, rather than taking the view that children need to be 'given' language. These views represent a more developmental theory of language and learning, one which sees learning as a steady and recursive series of experiences rather than as a set of separate 'skills' which can be put together like building bricks or as a straight line which can be measured by the 'quantity' of what has been learned. Those who hold to the 'building bricks' theory see learning as 'getting' rather than 'making' knowledge, and so are more likely to favour classroom practices which reflect this view in the quantity, rather than the quality, of children's writing. Other colleagues may find that they have conflicting views, suggesting that they still need to think through just what their theories about learning are. In order to make all of these possible standpoints clear, colleagues will need to open up some discussions about principles by following the list of 'what' is considered important with the question 'why':

Why are these things important:

- in the classroom?
- in the school?
- outside the school?

This can be a difficult move. It may be useful here to have some other people's ideas to consider, such as this refreshing view from the East Anglia LINC Consortium. In explaining that language is an important part of the environment, the co-ordinators point out:

> We teach children about all sorts of different aspects of the environment: about the air, about towns and cities, about plants and animals, about the weather. In the same way we need to teach them about language, for language isn't just part of the environment, it is also a medium through which we experience, interpret, and interact with that environment. Understanding language is an important part of understanding one's place in the world.[5]

Substitute 'writing' for 'language' and the statement still makes a lot of sense, and is an interesting way to think about constructing a writing curriculum.

These starting points for outlining principles and possible content for a writing curriculum will have already raised some critical questions about the writing policy as it is carried out daily in the classroom. As is often the case, when teachers need to sort out ideas they ask advice from their pupils. Teachers' own questions about classroom writing can be usefully amplified by some attempt at establishing how writing is perceived more generally by pupils themselves. These insights can then be followed by some practical guidelines based on shared views of just what matters about helping children feel confident about using writing.

Discover perceptions

Where the teachers at Burnham Copse started, and many other teachers, too, was to ask the children what they use writing for. This can be a startling experience but ends up as an enlightening and helpful way to start looking closely at writing in a school. As teachers we may be confident about the purposes of writing, but what do the pupils think and what do they already know about the forms and uses of writing? Their answers can shake us but at least they act as a kind of compass bearing to help us plot the route ahead. Are they, for instance, aware that their writing can do a job for them, or do they see it as fulfilling different intentions at school and at home?[6]

> What do children think they are writing for:
> - at home?
> - at school?
>
> What do the children know about writing?
> - What forms/genres are they familiar with?
> - What vocabulary do they use to describe texts?

Just as there is a growing emphasis on recognizing and valuing what the children bring to the classroom in terms of previous knowledge, so it is worth colleagues making clear to each other just what they know about how to organize a classroom for successful writing. Having begun to clarify some of the principles by asking and answering the questions 'What is important about children's writing? and 'Why are these things important?' and having started to find out what children think, the next question may be: How do we achieve these aims/ put these principles into practice? Or, more simply:

> What classroom experiences or activities do we provide to help children make progress with writing?

Recognize existing (good) practice

A list of activities, already happening, or on the agenda to be tried out, can be a most informative part of any school's policy for writing. In Burnham Copse the list included an interesting variety:

- writing to or for other pupils in the school
- writing to others outside the school
- making writing a specific focus for talk
- using different models and examples to stimulate writing
- keeping journals, both personal journals and work logs
- noticing how writing can be used in topic/science/CDT/maths
- using the word processor and desktop publishing
- inviting a visiting writer or poet
- responding to the meaning of writing rather than correcting for technical errors only
- trying out drafting and self-editing strategies
- developing ways of collaborating over writing

Setting up these activities, or describing those already happening, had an impact on the ways in which the teachers saw their role in the classroom. For some it was uncomfortable, but for others, the development of new ways of working gave them insights into just what their pupils could do. After a term's work on a CDT project which grew to include a whole variety of writing experiences, Sue Phillips wrote:

> The children's experiences have made me more aware of their untapped potential, their inventiveness, their willingness to learn from one another, and the variety of writing they are able to use.[7]

And Helen Maguire found that using a particular strategy for encouraging collaboration over redrafting work meant striking a sensitive balance between supportive intervention and a knowledge of when to stand back:

> In some cases my help was needed to encourage re-drafting. This sometimes involved just listening as the child read her/his story aloud. Often the child realised where additions and amendments were needed as they read to someone who listened attentively. At other times I had to ask specific questions when a child was dissatisfied with the story but felt they had 'finished'.[8]

Deciding on the 'how' of a policy, then, can be the biggest step in making explicit just what matters in classroom approaches to writing. Embarking on activities can lead to all sorts of unexpected consequences and give teachers and pupils experiences from which there is no turning back.

Review and evaluate

Once these activities are over, however, there is a need to evaluate just what they have meant in terms of children's progress as writers. For example, a single visit from a professional writer, in this case a poet, can reveal unexplored capacities in children as they write. Alexandra, aged 7, wrote a poem when Gareth Owen visited the school inspired by 'Come on in, the water's lovely':

Come on up
Come on up the view is lovely
Of course I won't push you down
There are men filling holes
Of course you won't fall
I am up here
There are cars and minibuses
You really will come up
On the count of three
One
It is really quite nice
Two
I will help you up
Three
Oh dear, Mummy's calling because it's tea
Just as you started climbing.

And Joanne, also aged 7, wrote after the visit:

> I thought Gareth Owen was a nice, funny man, and I thought his expressions were very funny. He made up good poems and his face was like jelly – always moving. His hair was like tangley bits of grey coloured wool . . .[9]

These showed their teachers just what very young children could do when given a stimulus which was based on contact with an adult writer for even a very short time during one day. The children's achievements established new parameters for thinking about how to evaluate children's writing. What was quite clear was that the opportunities offered make all the difference to the possibilities for progress. A series of questions to formulate what is offered might include:

> What classroom opportunities are offered for children to:
> - write in different ways?
> - read a variety of texts?
> - talk about writing?
> - collaborate over writing?
> - develop self-editing techniques?
> - see adults writing?
> - choose how and when to use writing in particular ways?

Gathering a list of these opportunities for writing becomes a spur to going further, perhaps involving children rather more in decisions about writing. Developing classroom practices for collaboration and partnerships for writing often makes it clear that children have greater capacities for self-evaluation than might have been imagined.[10]

Setting up the classroom conditions which will foster development in writing makes a policy real. The everyday experience gives the foundation for children to experience authentic and lasting success in writing. But for children's success to continue throughout the school there needs to be some agreement about the kinds of classroom approach which best support writing and the criteria by which writing may be judged to be successful. And this is where we began. Being able to describe, analyse and assess children's development as writers means that teachers need to have some agreed approach to how best to help children as writers and learners; some general view of what 'progress in writing' might look like. There needs to be a degree of consistency and continuity of approach. Working towards this may be the next step in sketching out the school's policy for writing. If teachers are to be able to agree on common aims and pass on to each other useful records of achievement in writing, then there will need to be agreement about how to identify and describe progress.

Focus on detail

The need to observe and record progress leads back to developing a way of looking closely and analytically at children's written texts to see just what they can do with writing. In order to show their capabilities to the full, children will need to demonstrate confidence in a range of writing tasks. To be able to do this they will need to have experienced writing in different forms and formats for a range of readers and for different reasons. The classroom as a literacy environment and the activities and experiences on offer will be critical factors in ensuring that assessments can be made over a suitably wide range of writing. Those parts of policy have already been mentioned. As well as considering the classroom as a supportive place for developing writing, other aspects need to be taken into account. If the classroom provides the backcloth for progress, the children's writing itself gives the detail. So there needs to be careful analysis of both text and context. Further to this, Katharine Perera adds an important note of caution. In writing about children's developing ability to handle the structures of written language, she emphasizes that this is only one aspect of learning to be a writer and therefore only one part of the teaching of writing:

> Good writing depends, first and foremost, on having something to write about; it requires from the writer such non-linguistic qualities as truthfulness, vigour, imagination and so on. It is quite possible for a piece of writing to contain varied vocabulary, mature sentence structures and well planned paragraphs and still be unsatisfactory because the writer was not committed to it.[11]

After considering the opportunities children have had for practising writing in different genres and for a range of readers, the focus will be on the texts themselves. Assessing just how children are developing as writers and learners will mean paying attention to particular features of children's written texts in order to determine how committed they seem to be, how successfully they have used writing to do the job they wanted it to do. Specifically, the kinds of questions worth asking might be:

- What was this text meant to do?
- Did the writer achieve her/his purpose?

- How effectively does it communicate with the reader?
- Does it show conviction and commitment?
- How successfully has the writer shaped and organized the material according to the intentions of the piece?
- What is the writer's level of technical competence?
- What knowledge of other texts does this reveal?

And then, if a full profile of a writer's capabilities is to emerge, these questions have to be applied to a variety of kinds of writing, for example:

- What range of texts can this writer handle?

And some note of writing behaviour has to be made:

How confidently does this writer:

- select a form appropriate for the job?
- choose to edit, revise and draft when needed?

As outlined earlier, an analytical framework like the one used in Chapter 2, applied to a selection of pieces over a year, expanded by comments about writing behaviour and supported by the writer's own evaluative comments, can give a full and informative outline of what a writer can do. It will prove an even more informative and helpful assessment document if it also gives some indication of where the writer might make improvements and progress further.

Record progress

Seen like this, describing progress becomes an integral part of planning for writing over a term or a year. As the school's writing policy is put into daily practice, so are the means of assessing how well the policy is working. The analysis of progress can only make sense in the context of what is happening in the classroom, and in this way assessment is necessarily bound up with every learning activity on offer. As was clear at the outset, disentangling the different threads of developing writing is a painstaking and slow process. Having spent some time on unravelling the separate strands, it is now time to put them together again to make the strong and varied texture of the school's writing policy. Beginning in the classroom, with the 'what' of a writing policy, then moving on to the 'why' and 'how', the interrelationships look like this:

1 Children can't make progress in writing unless they are given the classroom opportunities to experience texts in a variety of ways – reading them, talking about them, practising them in different forms and writing about them! For children to be able to write successfully, they need to *want* to write!
2 Assessment of progress in writing depends on the negotiated agreements between colleagues about what matters in children's writing.
3 Deciding what matters about writing depends on the experience of successful classroom practice which has given teachers a chance to see what helps children get better at writing.

4 Passing on useful information about children's writing development depends on the children having experienced a full range of writing opportunities, on teachers feeling confident in the shared criteria which they use to assess that writing, and on having a continuing and uncomplicated way of recording development.

In each case the principles which can be distilled as the 'headlines' of policy, for example, the importance of keeping and passing on records of progress, are embedded in everyday classroom practice. And we return full circle to the policy in action – the lived and living experience of writing as a means of developing confident and successful learners who can use writing not only as a means of making their own voices heard, but as a way of shaping and giving sense to their knowledge and experience of the world.

Put into a wider context

The three parts of the policy – content, practice and principles: 'what', 'how' and 'why' – are all built on and informed by a recognition of the value of those literacy and language experiences which the children bring with them from home. In this way, school, home and community work together to contribute to children's learning. There is a breadth of experience which needs to be drawn on if children are to make the most of the learning opportunities on offer. At the same time we know that the learning which goes on in one year in a classroom is part of a past and future picture of each child's development in writing and learning. Early school experiences and those which will follow until children leave full-time education – the depth of background – need also to be taken into account when putting a writing policy together. Looking at breadth and depth gives a fuller, two-dimensional view, but for the policy to be completely rounded and three-dimensional a width of experience needs also to be taken into account. By this we mean the wide range of curriculum areas which writing contributes to. In putting together these three dimensions, some of the questions worth considering might be:

- How do we give value and status to children's home language and literacy experience?
- How does our developing writing policy relate to other areas of school life?
- How does it fit with the school's equal opportunities policy?
- How does it inform other curriculum areas, especially those not traditionally associated with writing like PE, art, music, drama?
- How do we make our practices and principles about writing clear to parents, school governors and others?
- How do we usefully inform other teachers and other schools about those practices and the children's achievements?
- How can parents and others in the community become involved in writing?

Once writing becomes the focus for a fully three-dimensional approach, then the policy has really taken root. 'Going public' is the toughest test a policy can undergo but at the same time is probably the most helpful way of clarifying the practice and principles inherent in the policy. Having to explain ideas to others is one of the most effective ways of coming to understand something for ourselves. And since the policy forged through practice isn't just a set of densely typed pages, but evident in the books written by the children – the increased competence they show in redrafting and getting their writing 'right'; their ability to talk confidently and clearly about their own and others' writing – the evidence for that policy will be far more convincing and demonstrable than one written document can ever hope to show. The folders of children's writing will eloquently testify to progress and increasing capability in a way that test scores alone could never do.

The success of the school's policy for writing can be readily measured in a more informative and fruitful way if it is genuinely a policy in action. Encouraging participation from parents and others makes it finally clear what theoretical principles underlie the practice. Language is put firmly in the centre of children's continuing learning experience as the means not only of demonstrating knowledge but also of creating, forming and organizing that gradually accumulating knowledge through reading, writing, talking and listening. Writing is seen as inextricably linked with the other language modes, as embedded in a child's home and cultural experience, as part of a continuing story of the child's progress and as integral to all the learning opportunities on offer.

And is that the end of it, once the policy has evolved through this series of discussions, activities and experiences? The question hardly needs to be asked! No school, no community, is ever a fixed entity; its population, the views and insights held by its members, continually develop and move. What will not change will be the confident and firm knowledge of those who participated in the development of the policy that they have worked out for themselves about where they stand on children's language and learning. As one of the Burnham Copse teachers said after three years of looking closely at writing in her own classroom:

I'm just about ready to start now . . .

Notes

1 Both authors worked for three years on the National Writing Project which meant contact with colleagues in different parts of England and Wales.
2 Belinda Kerfoot-Roberts was involved with the work for several years and in 1989, with Yvonne Ryves, produced a set of materials about working with the microcomputer in the classroom, 'Simulations and Adventures: A Cross Curricular Approach', as part of a diploma course in Hampshire.
3 For a fully worked through analysis of the conditions helpful to teacher change, see M. Fullan, *The Meaning of Educational Change*, Columbia University, Teachers College Press (1982).

A WRITING POLICY IN ACTION

Start by talking

What is important about children's writing?

- about the writing itself?
- about how we respond to writing?
- about the classroom conditions to support writing?
- about the opportunities offered to help children get better at writing?
- about the kinds of writing we value most?
- about the different kinds of writing used throughout the curriculum?

Why are these things important:

- in the classroom?
- in the school?
- outside the school?

Discover perceptions

What do the children think they are writing for:

- at home?
- at school?

What do the children know about writing?

- What forms/genres are they familiar with?
- What vocabulary do they use to describe texts?

Recognize existing (good) practice

What classroom experiences or activities do we provide to help children make progress with writing? For example, have they:

- learned strategies for:
  planning information writing?
  starting off ideas/brainstorming?
  revising and editing?
  evaluating their own work?
  reflecting on language?
- made writing a specific focus for talk?
- experienced different models and examples to stimulate writing?
- tried keeping journals?
- been helped to notice how writing can be used in topic/science/CDT/maths?
- used the word processor and desktop publishing?
- ... and more can be added to this list ...

Review and evaluate

What classroom opportunities are offered for children to:

- use their existing language (and other) experience?
- write in different ways
  - for personal and communicative purposes?
  - briefly and more extensively?
  - to keep or to throw away?
- write for a variety of readers
  - in the class?
  - in the school?
  - outside the school?
- read a variety of texts
  - informational/persuasive/explanatory/narrative?
  - plays/poetry/novels/factual?
  - by children/by adults?
  - published nationally/locally/in the classroom?
- see writing in a variety of formats:
  - handwritten; typed/word-processed; desktop published?
  - in folders, books, scripts, comics, leaflets?
- talk about writing with
  - other children in the class?
  - other children in the school?
  - adults in school and out?
- talk about reading with
  - other children in the class?
  - other children in the school?
  - adults in school and out?
- develop a vocabulary through which to express ideas about texts?
- collaborate over writing with others
  - in the class?
  - in the school?
  - outside the school:
    - children?
    - adults?
- develop self-editing, drafting and revising techniques?
- see adults writing?
- choose how and when to use writing in particular ways?

Focus on detail and record progress

Looking at individual pieces can mean considering:

- What was this text meant to do?
- Did the writer achieve her/his purpose?
- How effectively does it communicate with the reader?
- Does it show conviction and commitment?
- How successfully has the writer shaped and organized the material according to the intentions of the piece?
- What is the writer's level of technical competence?
- What knowledge of other texts does this reveal?
- What information about writing should be passed on:
  - to the next class teacher?
  - to the next school?
- How can we involve children in the process?

Put into a wider context

How do we give value and status to children's home language and literacy experience?
How does our developing writing policy relate to other areas of school life?

- How does it fit with the school's equal opportunities policy?
- How does it inform other curriculum areas, especially those not traditionally associated with writing like PE, art, music, drama?

How do we make our practices and principles about writing clear to parents, school governors and others?
How do we usefully inform other teachers and other schools about those practices and the children's achievements?
How can parents and others in the community become involved in writing?

4 Help in clarifying ideas and setting an agenda can be found in Nelson/National Writing Project, *Making Changes*, Kingston, Nelson (1990), curriculum development materials.
5 From East Anglia LINC Consortium's leaflet 'Language in the National Curriculum', circulated in 1990.
6 There is a range of helpful suggestions for discovering what children think about writing in Nelson/National Writing Project, *Perceptions of Writing*, Kingston, Nelson (1989).
7 S. Phillips, 'Failing doesn't always matter' in Nelson/National Writing Project, *Writing and Learning*. Kingston, Nelson (1989).
8 H. Maguire, 'Collaboration' in *Hampshire Writing Project Newsletter*, autumn 1986.
9 Taken from C. Farrow, 'A writer visits' in Nelson/National Writing Project, *Writing Partnerships 1 – Home, School and Community*. Kingston, Nelson (1990).
10 Chapters 3 and 4 provided detailed examples of children's attentive and critical reading of their own writing arising from their use of the Writing Record Sheets. However, as can be seen in the journals quoted in Chapter 5, other ways can be found for children to use writing to assess their own progress in learning.
11 K. Perera, *Children's Writing and Reading*, Oxford, Basil Blackwell (1984), p. 208.

Appendix: Records of Achievement in Writing

The Record of Achievement in Writing for Andrew and Sally includes:

1 **A list of the different kinds of writing done during each term.** These are drawn from the children's writing books which they used for notes and early drafts. As pointed out in Chapter 4, one list will give the information needed for all the pupils in the class. If a child missed some of the writing, the copy in that child's file can be easily amended.
2 **Six pieces of writing (two per term) selected by the child, including the Writing Record Sheets compiled by the writers themselves and giving their reasons for selecting those pieces.** As explained earlier, the idea of the Writing Record Sheet evolved as the work was ending, so completed Writing Record Sheets are not included here, although there is a copy of the format at the end of the Appendix.

   The children's comments accompanying the selected pieces which follow are minimal since they were asked to choose six pieces of work they were most pleased with before we developed the format for the Record of Achievement in Writing. In a full Record, each piece of work would be accompanied by a completed sheet. One example of a completed sheet from another child is included as an example on p. 159.

   The six pieces in each of the 'folders' here could be used for colleagues to consider their own views of what each child can do with writing. We have added a few comments of our own to each piece.
3 **Six pieces of writing (two per term) selected by the teacher and commented on in the form of the analytical framework outlined in Chapter 2.** We have only included two pieces from each child here. In each case, in order to show development, one is drawn from early in the school year and one from much later.
4 **A Summary Sheet compiled by the teacher at the end of the year drawing on the comments in the file as well as classroom observations.**

RECORD OF ACHIEVEMENT IN WRITING: ANDREW P

Contents

1 List of some of the different kinds of writing completed during the year.
2 Andrew's six chosen pieces with teacher's comments.

   'The Magic Fireworks'
   'The Bear'
   Book Recommendation – *Eric The Viking*
   'Dr Doom's Adventures'
   'Disaster Came to the World'
   'Frankinstien II'

3 Two examples of Andrew's writing chosen by the teacher and commented on more fully.

   Poem – 'I'll tell you something . . .'
   Cinquain – 'Cheetah'

4 Summary Sheet

Section 1

Writing completed during the year included:

- chapters of a lengthy story
- some completed short stories
- poems in different forms including acrostics, haiku and cinquain
- drafts of letters – to an author, to some students who asked for book recommendations and to a friend who has left the school
- notes taken from a television programme about animals; notes from books about wildlife
- science experiments
- draft questions and an account of an interview with the local vicar
- brainstormed ideas while listening to music
- reflective writing about likes and dislikes
- comments by other children about the writer's latest work
- regular self-chosen spellings to concentrate on and practise
- writing in preparation for non-written outcomes – school assembly and the Pandora play.

Term One – November

Teacher's notes:

- writes in his own choice of comic book genre suggesting general sense of his peers as readers but with no real invitation to a reader

The magic fireworks
Hihgly excsplosive!!

The Magic Fireworks

One day on November the 5th I found some fireworks A Rocket, Sparkler and a Golden Rain squib. That night I went out and lit the sparkler. Suddunly a dassle of light went all over the Wolrd. Wow!...there Magic I said...The rocket was the biggest. There was a door in it I got in it. It zoomed! of 200 Rm. Then it landed with a sudden thump!
I still had the Golden Rain Squib in a box.

I planted the Golden Rain Squib and Real Gold came out! I went to a moter bike Shop. Gold! the owner said. I said can I buy a moterbike The owner said sure! I gave him a piece of gold. and took a yamaha 2000! I rode back home. ran up stairs and fell exeasted onto my bed.

- shapes the story by using the three named fireworks for the narrative thread
- varies sentence structure for effect
- knows how to use exclamation marks and rows of full stops for effect.

Term Two – January

The Bear.
A Poem about a hibernating bear.

The Bear.

Hibernates in the Winter does
the Bear
With lots of furry hair.
In the Spring he comes back
out
to catch some Trout!
He is so proud of his wood
like he really should.
He doesn't have a family
He hunts for himself
He is not the Winnie the Pooh
Because he doesn't have a
Honey Shelf.

Teacher's notes:
- chooses to use rhyming poem for factual information giving, though he breaks out of this at the end, loosening the rhyme where he moves to his experience of story/film
- doesn't need to acknowledge a reader as poetry is often written for a general readership
- organizes lines to fit with new elements of information
- some confusion over capitals but uses punctuation well.

Term Two – February

> Recomended Book.
> I added an excstreamly good drawing.
>
> what I like
>   about   Erik
> the Viking Story
>
> I like the story
> because eric takes
> his time and energy
> he goes through
> a lot of bother and he
> goes through a lot
> of adventures aswell
> I like all of the
> ideas the aulthor
> has put into it.

Unfortunately, the drawing hasn't survived.

Teacher's notes:

- gives clear reasons for choice
- writes for a generalized readership
- draws comments together with a summarizing sentence
- is developing a wider critical vocabulary
- is getting better at deciding where to use capital letters.

Term Two – March

Dr Doom's Adventures
I think it is a funny Well Written piece of writing.

Dr. Dooms Adventeres

One day in a far off land, there was a Dr "Doom" as called as there ruler. He made chemicals and posion, but no one could stop him, except one man, proctor dollite.

Dr. Doom	Proctor Dollite

One day proctor dollite was going for a walk when he met Dr. Doom. Dollite's glasses fell off! Dr. Doom was with his girlfriend "Samantha". Doom's cheeks went reder and reder until Doom fainted.

Proctor dollite made a sigh of relief, and went home. The next day proctor heard that Dr. Doom was in hospital. his next door neighbour. Mr. richs Van was stolen. So proctor went to see him in hospital. So off he went. on the way he met Samantha he said do you want a lift So to the hospital. Samantha said yes please. So proctor carryeid Samantha to the hospital. When they got there Doom punched proctor in the stomoch proctor had to stay in hospital, proctor said ill make a deal, you stop making poison and I gice you a fiver, you bet, said Doom, So they did then there they shared the there Choclate's between them!!! Just then the door burst open.... there was the nurse.

She was........
....Fat....ugly....mean....
.....greedy....Lazy.....
rude......and she's.....
Near to get the Sack. She was soofing a gigantic piece of Choclate cake get out of bed and make the, then draw the curtians!! then go home!! Dr. Doom got out of bed and tried to be Buck Rodgers! the nurse fled not forgeting the reamains of her choclate Cake,, Dr. Doom said i never did get the hang of Karate,, geting into bed with a broken leg and a black eye,, proctor was hiding his head under the pillows,, then in came samantha Hi! she said in a Shrilled Voice,, Hi! they said in a choras together,, They got out of bed push the nurse over and went home.

Teacher's notes:
- chooses comic book genre again – rather visual with gaps in the narrative suggesting cartoon/comic strip
- sets out to be humorous – to engage the reader
- will benefit from a reader's response to help clarity of story events
- capitals much more accurate now
- interesting experiments with punctuation
- poses the issue of how to discuss the (unnecessary?) violence with him.

Term Three – April

> Disaster Came to the World.
> The Thurropuss (half dog-half cat) Saved the World.

Disaster came to the World

Onl peace ful Summer day long long ago there lived a man called Judus and one night Jupiter sent a messenger (Mercury) ~~there~~ He said there will be a great storm because some one had ~~aferstbad the~~ smashed the bot of satisfactory. There will be death and life so shelter yourself. Dig a big set under the ground. There will be snow and frost, and insects that spread germs and disieses! So spread the news!!...It will come in four doys time. Here is a box. ~~Do not~~ open ~~the~~ it until the disarster comes. Then Mercury went. The desarster came causing caos. So Judus opened the box.

> and out jumped the ~~thur~~
> Thurropuss, half dog half
> cat.
>
> *(drawing of the Thurropuss with "Blow" and a figure)*
>
> The Thurropuss said, I am
> the Thurropuss, & have hope
> In me trust me, I have a
> very big blow! ~~he the~~ They
> went to the top of the passage
> going down to the set. ~~Thurr~~
> Thurropuss went and blew
> the storm away! ~~bet~~ but the
> germs and diesieses were
> still on the earth.

Teacher's notes:
- interesting choice of combining elements of known stories, both in the way the story is told and in the illustrations: the Bible; classical myth James Reeves poetry(?); comic strips
- has the cadences of a story to be told/read aloud
- clearer narrative thread than 'Dr Doom' – interesting to speculate why . . .
- language echoes the dignified/serious tone of the story
- is using punctuation with much greater confidence.

138 WRITING POLICY IN ACTION

Term Three – May

Frankinstien II.
Frankinstein is trying to be famous!

Frankinsien II

One dark night in the town of ?? Frankinstien!! there was Frankinstien!......2!!

Now we come to the End! Oh! I mean the story. Frankinsien was glum! he was sick of being called Frankie! Then he had an idea he would get an idea!! What a brilliant idea. he went outside and made a sign saying Ideas, everybody thought it was a shop and came in; there was a sign saying upstairs for the dead room instead of bedroom they went up - in to the dead room, & they went in and saw a coffin, they looked in expecting to see clothes, but saw Frankinstien he said close the lid mate. Ta! Wait a minute you came to see me...............

I'm Famous!! he shouted and lived happily ever after!!

Bye!

Teacher's notes:

- is he getting stuck in a too familiar genre?
- is developing humour/irony nicely, writing to engage the reader: 'Now' 'Oh! I mean...'
- again a 'visual' approach to the narrative but rather more cohesive than before
- highly varied and impressive sentence openers and structure
- increasing sureness of punctuation and spelling.

APPENDIX 139

Section 3 Teacher's chosen pieces

Term One – October

I'l tell you something ~~that~~
that happened to me
I ~~wetw~~ent to the phone
to give my ~~a~~ nan a ring.
~~a ring~~ || and I Waited...
and Waited || I put down the Phone
~~phone~~
and I told my mum || She was not in
She told me to do it agian
~~agian~~ so I Went in to the hall
~~hall~~ in a bad mood
I Shouted out ~~t~~
to ~~number took in the~~
~~to~~ my mum || What is her
number? || shut up and phone her
~~her~~. I went to the Kitchen
~~the Kitchen~~ and I WENT
OUT! || Shutting the door
with a great BIG
~~big~~ SLAM!
a few minutes later

I came back in
I said I was ~~going~~ going
for a bike ride
and my mum went

hmmm......
come on I said
She didn't answer
So I went out
on my.....
....BiKE.

Teacher's fuller analysis:

Choices/intentions
- selects a particular – and dramatic – everyday incident to shape into a poem
- fulfils the genre requirement of the task as set by the teacher.

Awareness of reader
- makes an immediate link with readers: 'I'll tell you'
- writes in an amusing way about a familiar situation which at the time was highly emotionally charged; he knows that others can appreciate this kind of incident with the amused detachment of hindsight.

Form/organization
- redrafts to present his ideas in the most effective places, using line endings and variation to emphasize points
- confidently rearranges, deletes or leaves the text alone
- has effectively used his knowledge of how other writers put texts together.

Technical features
- uses capitals and rows of full stops for effect
- has few problems with conventional spellings
- identifies and corrects errors with help.

Could work on

General punctuation. Obviously he knows how to punctuate sentences, but needs to be helped to self-correct when he has missed full stops.

APPENDIX

Term Three – June

Andrew's original notes taken from a television programme:

> Attack and defence
> A Cheetah was after a gazzele., the gazzele dodged to defend. the cheetah was out of breath and gave up. the gazelle may knot be as fast as the cheetah.. But is as cunning The Trap-door spider waits in its tube until its prey is close. then it strikes.. grabs the prey and goes down the tube.. kills the prey and eats it.

Led to:

> Cheetah
> A ~~##~~ carnivore runs swiftly to its ~~prey~~ lunch pulls it down the prey is ~~hopeless~~ Feasting!!

142 WRITING POLICY IN ACTION

Teacher's fuller analysis:

Choices/intentions

- fulfils his own intentions entirely by choosing an expressive form for his view of information drawn from a factual source
- has confidently completed the task.

Awareness of the reader

- has no clearly identified reader indicated in the text although he knows that anybody in the class might read it.
- has achieved the most difficult task – a piece written for all. (This is what published poets do!)

Form/organization

- follows the cinquain form accurately
- uses its economy to make maximum impact.

Technical features

- writes a clear and confident first draft
- spells accurately
- shows, by his editing that he has made a conscious choice about how best to express his ideas by avoiding repetition.

Could work on

General punctuation – still!

APPENDIX 143

Section 4   Summary sheet at end of year

Writing Profile   *Andrew P*   *Year 4*

Choices/intentions

Over the year Andrew has:

- developed his confidence to write in different forms
- become highly competent in shaping poems
- experimented with humorous genres for story
- become assured about choosing how he will write
- enlarged his range of formats to include diagram and illustration.

Awareness of reader

Andrew can:

- adapt his writing to suit different readers by including relevant information and using appropriate register
- go beyond this to write for a completely unknown 'general public'
- decide when and how to involve readers in what he writes
- use humour to entertain.

Form/organization

Andrew has:

- a clear sense of how to arrange short texts, for information, giving an opinion or expressing himself through poetry
- developed a wide range of organizational devices – arrows, diagrams, flow charts, etc.
- made some effective notes.

Technical features

Andrew has:

- developed a sound method for practising spellings
- been consistently able to edit and revise his own work with and without help
- shown the ability to vary sentence structure
- demonstrated competent use of: full stops, commas, exclamation marks, question marks, apostrophes of omission and possession.

Could work on

- Different genres for writing
- Story structure
- Sentence boundary marking.
- More practice in note-making.

RECORD OF ACHIEVEMENT IN WRITING: SALLY W

Contents

1 List of some of the different kinds of writing completed during the year.
2 Sally's six chosen pieces with teacher's comments.

>Candle – Science
>Planet writing (a letter)
>Haiku (about Alice)
>Pandora work (a theatre) (and writing)
>'The apple with 400 Eyes' (a story)
>'Looking at an animal' (cat)

3 Two examples of Sally's writing chosen by the teacher and commented on more fully.

>'The Magic Fireworks'
>'The apple with 400 Eyes'

4 Summary Sheet.

Section 1

Writing completed during the year included:

- chapters of a lengthy story
- some completed short stories
- poems in different forms including acrostics, haiku and cinquain
- drafts of letters – to an author, to some students who asked for book recommendations and to a friend who has left the school
- notes taken from a television programme about animals; notes from books about wildlife
- science experiments
- draft questions and an account of an interview with the local vicar
- brainstormed ideas while listening to music
- reflective writing about likes and dislikes
- comments by other children about the writer's latest work
- regular self-chosen spellings to concentrate on and practise
- writing in preparation for non-written outcomes – school assembly and the Pandora play.

Term Two – January

Candle ~~Scence~~ scinerce

It was about a sort of progect we did with our teacher about a kind of science and ~~efer to~~ after we had done it we had to write about it.

I liked my peice of writing because I discribed it quite well and people could understand it.

what we have got.
We've got a jar, a plastic container and a candle which has been stuck with bluetack in the container and some ~~mathe~~ matches, Then ~~we~~ Mrs Farrow lit the candle and then we covered the candle with the Jar it took 9½ seconds to go out it had gone out because there ~~was~~ no oxygen in the Jar. When we took the Jar off it had left a little black mark on the Jar because it had burned. The next time we lit and covered it, it took 10 seconds to go out. We did it another time and it took 15 seconds Then we did it another time and it took 8 seconds Then we put a bigger bit over the candle it took a bit longer to go out because there was more oxygen in the Jar because it was bigger. The First one took 13 seconds and so did the third one but the Second and last one took 12 seconds.

Teacher's notes:
- gives clear explanation of materials and equipment
- well-observed details
- organized chronologically
- ready to move on to setting out tabular notes
- clearly marked sentences, though repetitive sentence openers.

Term Two – February

> Planet Writing (a letter)
> I was pleased with it because I think I discribed well and you can imagine what the planet looks like.
>
> Planet Picture letter
> I am on the planet and I landed safley The planet looks familier and the creatures have got two heads! We made friends with the creatures slowly and they showed us around. their was a talking shark, an octupus with 6 legs and a rat with such a long tail you could slide down it! When we got out of the spaceship the creatures showed surprise by opening their eyes wide and falling back on to the floor. They eat by lying down on their tummys and wiggeting round on the floor and eating! It is quite funny to watch them. What they eat is Superduperpuperdragon food.
> They showed fear by getting on their knees and fainting! It is quite exciting. Wish you were here love Sally.

Teacher's notes:

- responds to the ideas suggested for details: 'how do they show surprise?', etc., reflected in text
- lively, engaging humour with reader appeal
- more varied sentence openers
- accurate and varied punctuation.

Term Two – March

> <u>Haiku</u> (~~Abot~~ about Alice)
>
> I liked this Haiku because it said clearly and made it sound real
>
> <u>My Haiku</u>
> Alice fell asleep
> 'Oh my tails and whiskers'
> Said the White rabbit

Teacher's notes:
- written for her own pleasure
- as Sally says, it is clear – a 'cameo' of the story
- perfect haiku form, showing awareness of how to use syllables, lines, economical language
- accurate speech punctuation
- delightful!

Term Two – March

Pandora Work (a Theatre) (and writing)

We did a theatre for Pandora work and we tried to raise some money for the guide class. ~~the~~ in the end we raised £8.9p and I was really pleased but it was the writing I was quite pleased with.

Pandoras ~~blue~~ silver box

One day ~~many~~ ~~i'~~ many years ago when the sky was blue with no clouds, the grass was green and everybody was happy, no ~~figh~~ fighting, no illness or disease and no troubles. One day two brothers called Prometheus and Epimetheus ~~were~~ were tott in ~~the~~ thier cottage talking when Prometheus said "I must go and pack and leave, but here is one ~~a~~ warning do not receive any gifts from the gods for somebody is after me", for Prometh~~etos~~eus had stolen fire ~~from~~ from Mercury. Prometheus left and Epimetheus waved goodbye as Prometheus set off down the hard road. Later that day there was a rat-a-tat-tat on the door, Epimetheus opened it and infront of him ~~there~~ there was a man with a beutiful beautiful lady in a pretty gown. "I am the god Mercury and have brought you this this gift, her name is Pandora". Mercury went away and left Pandora with Epimetheus. Epimetheus couldn't help resiting on having such a ~~be~~ pretty lady. Next morning there was ~~a~~ ~~a~~ another knock on the door, and Pandora rat-a-tat-tat-tat. Epimetheus opened it and ~~there~~ was a man who's name was

APPENDIX 149

Jupiter. "This is a gift from all the gods," said Jupiter and handed Epimetheus and Pandora a silver box. "There is ~~the~~ 1 warning you must never open this box for it could bring unhappiness to you." Jupiter went and on a few weeks ~~later~~ later when Epimetheus was out picking strawberries on the hill Pandora was getting more and more curios ~~about the~~ about the little silver box. In the end she took it down from the shelf and said "that's it I've had ~~on~~ enough ~~ov~~ I'm looking" Pandora turned the little key and ~~o~~opened the box a teeny weeny bit ~~but~~ and all these little winged insects came out and they stung her from head to toe and brushed against her face but, at last, the troubles flew out the window. Then a little butterfly came out of the silver box "my name is Hope," said the butterfly "I will go and try and fight all the troubles but it won't be easy." So Hope flew ot of the window and did try to and fight them but ~~there~~ although there is illness and unhappiness there is always hope.

Teacher's notes:

- follows the genre well, retelling the heard story clearly
- writes for a reader as well as a hearer, as when she uses recognizable literary devices: trail of full stops after 'such a pretty lady . . .'
- clear narrative structure: sets the scene with good visual detail; weaves in past and continuous present, using variation of tense confidently and consistently
- increasingly accurate – and adventurous – punctuation
- varied and sophisticated sentence structure, particularly in use of openers and conjunctions.

Term Three – April

<u>The apple with 400 eyes (a story)</u>

~~My friends~~ I was pleased with it because we made it short and exciting and described well and not long and boring.

The ~~Apple~~ apple with 400 eyes.

One day ~~is~~ two ~~s~~ sisters called Sally & krisy were playing in there bedroom when — suddenly ~~Blu Blu~~, Blu Blu Blu Blu Blu Bluu ~~some~~ suddenly this kind of song came out in a chinese kind of way the ~~thing~~ apple ~~xx~~started to sing "I am the apple with 400 eyes, I like to sing and I like to cry, I like to whispop day and night sooo ooo o ooooo ooooooooo I am the apple with four hundred eyes," Sally & said "who are you"? The apple said "come out into the garden and I will tell you," they went down to the garden and the apple said "my name is pickle face and I am a big rosy apple" * "ohooh", said sally & krisy "why do you have all all allallMMMMMMM those eyes. "Because they are allMMMMMM wishes" said pickle face — "Oh can we make some wishes," said the girls. "Oh yes," said pickle face. "Oh can we make one now," said krisy "yes," said pickle face. "Oh my" said Sally "what shall we wish krisy?", "But," said pickle face "you have to sing this song before you wish, this is it,"

"BANNNNANNA lou lou lou lou lou lou lou lou lou BANNNANNA lou lou loulou lou BANNNANNA I wish to go to .... Thats what you have to sing", Sally began "BANNNANNA lou lou lou lou lou BANNNANNA loulou lou lou lou BANNNANNA lou lou bu BANNNANNA I wish to go to the land of mars bars... AND then Krisy began to sing BANNNANNA etc... To the land of lollipops......

SUDDENLY lots of flashing lights come and ████████

a sound came from the window sill ✳✳ ✳✳✳ which was what the sound was coming from. With 400 eyes.

See Section 3 (below) for comments.

Term Three – April

<u>looking at an animal (Cat)</u>

I was pleased with it because I discribed it well

Looking at an Animal
<u>Fatty a Cat</u>

on it's coat there are the colours black brown orangey browny and a bit of whitey-grey. The markings on its coat are sort of white striks inbetween its fur. It has got legs & it moves about by moving either 2 legs or 1 legs at a time. It hasn't got wings. It Uses part of his body to move, its shoulders and sometimes its back moves up and down. It doesn't have use its tail to move. It moves like a big cat except its shoulders don't move up & down so much. It has got eyes. Its eyes are sort of in the same place as ours. I think the eyes look the same way. He has got 2 eyes. His eyes are sort of a grey yellowy colour. It eats like a licking it up then chewing it. It laps when it

APPENDIX 153

> drinks. ~~His~~ Its mouth is beneath his nose. It eats catfood called Kitecat, normaly on the kitchen floor, sometimes outside. Yes it has got ears. They are on the top of its head by the side. They are about 4 cms long. Yes is has got a nose. The nose is just above the mouth. Its nose is a pinky colour. Its nose is quite dry it is about 1 cm long. His coat feels soft. It has 4 legs. It has got paws on the end of its legs. ~~(It is a cat.)~~ It is quite a bumpy shape. He is about 16 inches long. I don't know how much it ~~wayys~~ weighs. Yes it has got bones.

Teacher's notes:

- fulfils the task given by providing well-observed 'scientific' description
- keeps well within the requirements of this kind of task, using no unnecessary or 'lyrical' description
- writes for the teacher to read: answers the questions given – for example, 'Yes, it has got bones'
- follows the structure dictated by the questions
- less varied sentence structures with particularly repetitive openers, although this is almost inevitable, given that the task was to note biological details
- accurate spelling and punctuation.

Section 3 Teacher's chosen pieces
Term One – November

~~My~~ The magic Fireworks.

Once upon a ~~time a go~~ there was a little girl called lisa and it was her birthday the very next day. In bed she was thinking about what she would get. ~~She t She was also thinking about what it would be like to be 9~~ Would she get some fireworks? It was near bonfire night, her mum might think she was to small to handle huge fireworks. Anyway she would'nt get fireworks for a birthday present or would she?

Next morning she opened all her presents and then dad came in and handed her a big hevy box, " from grandma I think" said dad "I can recognise her handwriting".

lisa eagerly opened the box then she shouted ~~what~~ with glee " FIREWORKS grandma sent me fire works".

Mum and dad said "tonight we must have a very big bonfire and set these fireworks off".

In the box there were sparklers and rockets and two golden rains.

That night when mum and dad were still washing up lisa slipped outside and ~~and~~ sat on a step looking at them. ~~She~~ lisa had sneaked some matches aswell she lighted one of the sparklers it went out as soon

as she lit it, she tryed another one and another and another untill only 1 was left.
"I had better keep that one it looks just a bit ~~strange~~ strange she hid in her trouser pocket.
Mum and dad came out then and lit one golden rain dad picked it up to light but just as he was going to lisa said "keep that plese dad keep it" So dad said he would. When he did the rockets she said the same thing. Lisa felt something very strange about all ~~of~~ them.

The next day she asked her ~~sate~~ mum if she could take a packed lunch and go out her mum said she could.

Lisa went to the woods and she had taken her ~~~~ 3 fireworks with her. Lisa sat down against a tree to have her lunch then suddenly she fell back and she looked up and saw a nasty looking witch looking down at her.
" lots of people fall down my little hole you cannot escape from here there are not any windows in this house.
oh no! thought lisa I cant get out but lisa was still thinking about the 3 fireworks she had still got them when the witch took her up to a cell lisa thought and took out a knife she had. She then carved a little window and put the rockets on her back she pulled a string on the rocket and suddenly she zoomed out. He

> window and was home.
> "I'm back mum" lisa said.
> "but do you mind if I go to bed.
> The next day *night* she lit the sparkler and it went so bright the it was day for a whole hour. then the next night she lit the golden rain and her mum and dad and lisa watched in amazment at all the gold wich came pouring out. ~~They~~ Then they became very rich and lisa really thankinged ~~it~~ her grandma really very much for those really magic fireworks
> THE END

Teacher's fuller analysis:

Choices/intentions

- tells a coherent story appropriate to the suggested title
- reflects in her writing some of the elements of books she has read where the girl is the central character, and magic and witches abound!

Awareness of reader

- starts in a recognized story-telling form, anticipating a readership or an audience for a told/read-aloud story
- uses questions and a colloquial register (for example, repeating 'really') to invite reader participation.

Form/organization

- uses the content (three chosen fireworks) to shape the narrative; each is used precisely for its particular qualities
- keeps the story coherent, making the ending fit with the beginning by thanking grandma.

Technical features

- can use speech punctuation accurately

- varies sentence openers
- uses the language of known story (for example, 'with glee').

Could work on

Sally could look more carefully at the internal structure of her stories as the middle of this one rather strays from a clear line, but generally she has a good foundation to build on.

Term Three – April

The apple with 400 eyes – full text included on pages 150–1.

Teacher's fuller analysis:

Choices/intentions

- decides on a magic story with girls as central characters
- chooses to make her story funny – even zany – by selecting her preferred form, content and tone
- succeeds in writing something to amuse or entertain.

Awareness of the reader

- involves the reader by humour
- shows a very keen sense of what the story would sound like if read aloud
- makes amendments to include information a reader needs to make sense of the story.

Form/organization

- has an awareness of a clear overall structure – this is a first draft
- constructs a coherent line of incidents within a 'magic' genre; there is nothing extraneous in this story
- knows that stories do not need closures to make them interesting; in fact, she chooses to leave this story as a cliffhanger.

Technical features

- uses punctuation confidently and enthusiastically
- creates 'special effects' with both punctuation and language, adding humour and vitality; plays with language and sound for fun – 'whispop'
- spells and punctuates accurately overall, especially as this is a first draft; has developed her own system for revising her text.

Could work on

Stories in a different genre. She does tend to use humour, magic and girls frequently! Will need some structured help to break new ground.

Section 4 Summary sheet at end of year

Writing profile   **Sally W**   **Year 4**

Choices/intentions

Sally has shown that she can:

- write competently in a wide range of forms both when she is writing to someone else's brief or when she chooses for herself
- select content for informational and factual material and write it clearly and concisely
- write serious and comic poetry very effectively
- use humour and illustration well in extended narrative.

Awareness of reader

Sally can:

- amuse, inform, entertain and persuade readers
- use an appropriate tone and register for different occasions
- select information necessary for particular readers.

Form/organization

Sally has:

- particular ability in organizing factual information
- experimented with differing ways of using the same information
- developed a system for reorganizing text
- gained confidence and competence in organizing lengthy narrative (her writing book contains several chapters of a long story)

Technical features

Sally can:

- self-edit and revise independently
- use commas, full stops, exclamation marks, question marks, speech punctuation, apostrophes of omission and possession accurately and consistently
- select vocabulary effectively; invent words for particular effects; play with language to create atmosphere
- vary sentence length, openers and connectives to suit her intentions.

Could work on

- experiments with more varied genres for extended narrative (see notes on 'The apple with 400 Eyes')
- developing and using her obviously good ear for language
- trying out more formats for writing, developing her ability to write notes, use diagrams, etc.

EXAMPLE OF COMPLETED WRITING RECORD SHEET

Record Sheet

Name:

Title: pandoras box

Date: May 5th

What I was Pleased with: the bit I was plesad with was when she fidled with the key and it opened

What I'd like to do better: I wold like to make it better by putting l little bit more exting bits in

What other people said: Alex said he liked the bit when pandora was shocked.

Teacher's Comments The sort of opening you would expect from this kind of story. It sets the scene and tells us that the world was peaceful. Your ending is a good one which explains the point of the story. You kept the reader in mind. Two improvements: you could have described the appearance of the box. You could have put in more detail of the troubles that the insects caused. You marks your sentences correctly... most of the time! Capital "P" sits on the line!

Index

Adams, A., 114n
Arnold, R., 57n
Assessment, 22–4, 36–7, 55, 57n, 76–7

Barrs, M., 25n
Bleich, D., 105, 113n
Bruner, J., 13, 19, 20, 21, 22, 25n, 105
Burnham Copse Junior School, 24n, 25n, 115, 119, 125

Christie, F., 102–3, 113n
Cohen, R., 105, 113n
collaboration over writing, 19, 20–2, 59–60, 70–71, 106, 107, 120, 121
Couture, B., 25n, 95n, 113n, 114n
Cox Report (*English for Ages 5 to 16*), 60, 75n, 104, 113n
culture and writing, 20–2

DES (TGAT Report), 9, 25n, 76, 95n
drafting, 46–8, 84–6, 117, 120

Edwards, D., 21, 26n
evaluation, 22–4, 69–75, 120–1

Foucault, M., 114n

genre
    children's knowledge and use of, 24, 59, 61, 68, 75, 86–95, 97, 108
    conventions, 51–2, 99
    definition of, 13
    teaching genre forms, 103–7

Hampshire Writing Project, 128n
Hansen, J., 22, 25n, 26n

ILEA Primary Language Record, 8–9, 25n
intervention, 15–16, 18–19, 55, 107

journals, 107–13, 128n

language
    diversity, 24n
    knowledge about (KAL), 13–16, 19, 95, 96–113
Language in the National Curriculum (LINC)
    East Anglia, 118, 128n
    North London, 25n, 113n

Macquarie University, 8
Martin, J. R., 95n, 103, 104–6, 113n, 114n
Mercer, N., 21, 26n
Moss, G., 52, 57n

National Curriculum
    Attainment Targets for Writing, 3, 7, 10, 11, 13, 14, 18, 23, 25n, 36, 75n, 95, 95n
    Non-Statutory Guidance for English, 82, 83, 84, 95
National Curriculum Council, 82, 95n
National Writing Project, 24n, 25n, 56n, 57n, 62, 105, 114n, 125n, 128n

Pereira, K., 122, 128n
Peters, P., 7–8, 25n
poetry, 61–2, 84, 87
Primary Language Record, 8–9, 25n
punctuation, 12–13, 17, 57, 59, 86, 87

reading, 61, 108–9
  children reading their own writing, 19, 77n
  teachers as readers, 62–9
record keeping, 57n, 72, 78–95, 97, 123–4
response partners, 63–9, 74, 114n
Richmond, J., 13–14, 15, 16, 20, 25n, 97, 113
Rosen, M., 84
Rothery, J., 95n, 103, 104–6, 113n, 114n

Sawyer, W., 113n
self evaluation, 55, 60, 69–75, 82, 121
Somerset ('Write to Learn' Project), 114n
spelling, 12–13, 57n, 86
Stallard, K., 25n
Styles, M., 20, 25n
syntax, 12–13, 17, 57

teacher
  as facilitator, 60–2
  intervention, 15–16, 18–19, 55, 107
  role, 18–19, 24
TGAT (Task Group on Assessment and Testing; DES), 9, 25n, 76, 95n

vocabulary, 12–13, 57n, 60, 61, 97
  technical, 109–10
Vygotsky, L. S., 21, 26n, 27

Wallen, M., 8, 25n
White, J., 105–6, 114n
Wiltshire Write to Learn Project, 25n, 114n
writing
  apprenticeship, 68
  audiences for, 8, 61, 62–9, 77, 122
  awareness of reader, 29–56, 57, 86–95
  children as evaluators, 69–75
  choice, 29–56, 57n, 77n, 82n, 86–95n
  collaborative writing, 19n, 20–2, 59–60n, 70–1n, 106–7n, 120n, 121n
  computers and writing, 48n, 116n
  content, 48–52n
  culture and writing, 20–2
  development, 27–9n
  disposable writing, 36, 41–3
  environment for writing, 58n, 77n, 117n
  form, 29–56n, 57n, 86–95, 102
  formats for writing, 77, 119–20, 122
  journals, 107–13
  logs, *see* journals
  models for writing, 60
  partnerships for writing, 20–2, 25n, 121
  perceptions of writing, 5–8
  policy, 76–7, 102, 107, 115–25
  profile, 93–4, 143, 158
  purposes for writing, 62–9, 77n, 119, 122
  record of achievement, 82–95, 95n, 96, 129
  record sheet, 72, 83–4, 95n, 98–103, 113n, 128n, 129, 159
  reflective writing, 57n, 107–13
  response to writing, 63–9, 77, 107–8, 117